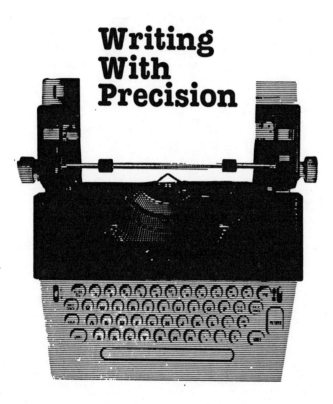

Writing
With
Precision

Writing With Precision

How To Write
So That You
Cannot Possibly
Be Misunderstood

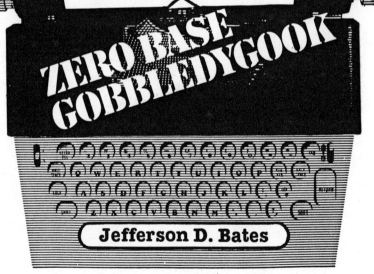

ZERO BASE
GOBBLEDYGOOK

Jefferson D. Bates

Illustrated by

Phil Kromas

PUBLISHED BY ACROPOLIS BOOKS LTD. • WASHINGTON, D.C. 20009

ACROPOLIS BOOKS LTD.
Colortone Building, 2400 17th St., N.W., Washington, D.C. 20009

Printed in the United States of America by
COLORTONE PRESS Creative Graphics, Inc.
Washington, D.C. 20009

Library of Congress Cataloging in Publication Data
Bates, Jefferson D., 1920-
  Writing with precision.
  Bibliography: p.
  Includes index.
  1. Exposition (Rhetoric) 2. English language—
Rhetoric. 3. Editing. I. Title.
PE1429.B35   808'.042   78-1924
ISBN 0-84791-184-2
ISBN 0-87491-185-0 pbk.

Dedication

To Mr. B and Susie,
who first inspired my love for the English language.

Table
of Contents

PART ONE

1. INTRODUCTION

2. THE CRAFT OF THE EDITOR

10. KNOW YOUR AUDIENCE

11. GETTING AND HOLDING THE READER'S ATTENTION

12. HOW TO DO "HOW-TO-DO-ITS"

13. HOW TO WRITE REGULATIONS

14. HOW TO WRITE REPORTS

15. HOW TO WRITE LIKE A PROFESSIONAL

PART TWO

HANDBOOK SECTION

PART THREE

ADDITIONAL EXERCISES, by Louis J. Hampton

ANSWERS TO EXERCISES

Preface to the Fourth Edition

When the original edition of this book was published in 1978, a lot of things were different. George ("Winning is everything") Allen was coach of the Washington Redskins, sometimes known in those days as the "over-the-hill gang." Telly Savalas (whom I admire because we look so much alike from the ears up) was starring in "Kojak," a big hit on prime time TV. Peanuts were popular. And I still qualified (barely) as middle-aged.

Some things, of course, were much the same as they are now. People were complaining about high prices. And taxes. And government forms that nobody could read.

Writing With Precision was my first commercially published book under my own by-line. (Until then, I'd spent most of my career ghostwriting). My hope was that it might sell a few hundred copies. My publisher, Al Hackl, knowing the realities about books by unknowns, may well have had even lower expectations. Still, he was bravely willing to take the risk.

Both of us were happily surprised when WWP (as we now affectionately call it) was selected by four book clubs. This, plus good reviews, sent it into additional printings and eventually into revised editions. This makes four.

That's why I have the pleasant task of writing this new preface. It's time to revise outdated references. (After all, I wasn't concerned about putting topical items in the book when I wrote it; I thought it would be out of print before it was out of date. My friend Carl Sieg, a management consultant, read the manuscript and suggested I take them out. I thought he was crazy.)

Figuring out what topical references to update hasn't always been easy. For example, George Allen. He hasn't coached the Redskins for years, but he's still dedicated to winning. So my references to him on pages 42 and 151 remain unchanged.

Take the number of books that Isaac Asimov has written (page 130). I've changed the "more than 200" to "more than 300" to be deliberately vague, in spite of my usual efforts to be precise. This is simple self-preservation. Dr. Asimov keeps turning them out so fast there is no way I can keep up. Sorry about that.

On a more personal level, the text continues to refer to my memtors, Mazie (Rodgers) Worcester and James R. Aswell as if they were still living. That's author's privilege. They remain very much alive in my mind and heart.

It was Mazie who told me, when I was a fledgling technical editor, "Don't believe *anybody.*" The highest compliment she ever paid me was "That's not so worse." But when she died in 1980, she bequethed me her beloved "Second Edition" of the big Merriam-Webster Unabridged. I cherish it.

Jim Aswell, my best friend and toughest editor, died in a retirement home in California. I called him one Sunday afternoon in 1982 when he didn't respond to a letter I'd written a few weeks earlier. A woman at the desk answered the phone, and when I asked for him, she broke the news bluntly. "He's dead."

Then she softened a little. "Oh, you're the one who came to see him last year."

"That's right."

"He talked about you sometimes," she said. "I guess maybe you'd like to know he was holding a book in his hand when he died."

Lately I've been appreciating more than ever the good fortune I've had in working with great friends and mentors. I know now that it's important to pass out bouquets while people can still smell the roses. I'll never get a better chance to acknowledge my debt. A couple of summers ago a famous surgeon overhauled my heart, which had become slightly the worse for wear. He installed a new technological gadget—I love gadgets—a fancy plastic-and-metal aortic valve. Pepped me up quite a bit. Sometimes it gets a little noisy, but I'm happy to listen to it.

My idea of the good life is to keep on leading seminars and writing books. It's much easier since I learned to dictate the first drafts. I even dictated a book about that. *(Dictating Effectively,* Acropolis, 1981.) Jim Aswell and several others whose opinions I respect told me it's a better book than WWP, but you probably haven't run across it in your neighborhood bookstore. Maybe it's because of the title, which doesn't sound very exciting. In retrospect, I should have called in something like "Writing Out Loud," or "Writing With a Tape Recorder," since it's as much about writing as it is about dictation.

My aim, as it was before, is to teach according to the marvelous admonition of Robert Louis Stevenson: "Don't write merely to be understood. Write so you cannot possibly be misunderstood."

Back in 1978, in the first edition of WWP, I employed a variation of Stevenson's theme as the book's subtitle: "How to Write So You Cannot Possibly Be Misunderstood." I intend to keep on using it—not, however, without the same disclaimer I used then. It goes like this:

> It's a marvelous thought, and I like it very much. But while I hope it sells a lot of books, I also hope it doesn't do so under false pretenses. Heaven knows *I* can't write so that I cannot possibly be misunderstood, so it's unlikely I can teach you. Still, I can't think of anything I'd rather shoot for. Even trying is worth something; actually, it's worth quite a lot.

I still believe that. After you've read this book, I hope you will too.

Jefferson D. Bates
Speak/Write Systems, Inc.
P.O. Box 3445
Fairfax, VA 22038
    14 September 1984

Don't write merely to be understood.
Write so you cannot possibly be misunderstood.
—Robert Louis Stevenson

Credo

I BELIEVE that writers have responsibilities to their readers. The first of these responsibilities is never to waste the readers' most valuable commodity—time. The second, closely related and just as important, is to strive diligently to write clearly, concisely, and PRECISELY.

I BELIEVE that anyone in business or government who writes documents affecting the lives of the public has a special obligation to honor these responsibilities.

I BELIEVE that anyone willing to expend the effort can learn to write plain English that says what it means and means what it says.

That's what this book is all about.

> *The man is most original who can adapt*
> *from the greatest number of sources.*
>
> —*Thomas Carlyle (1795-1881)*

Acknowledgments

If Thomas Carlyle was correct, I must be a very original writer. This treatise owes a debt to "every book I've ever read and every person I ever knew." Even that statement is "borrowed"—straight from Bergen Evans' acknowledgments for his *Dictionary of Quotations.* Where better could one lift a quote?

English majors are always told that "borrowing from one book is plagiarism, while borrowing from many is scholarship." By this definition, *WRITING WITH PRECISION* is a scholarly work. For more than a quarter of a century I've been collecting books on writing, style, composition, rhetoric, grammar, and related subjects. Over the years they have gradually mixed together like a rather untidy English pudding. Thus, when I began to track down the sources of many of the ideas in this book, it took considerable detective work. Any lack of success is not because of a corresponding lack of effort.

For the record, when borrowing well-known phrases from equally well-known writers, which I am occasionally wont to do, it seems a bit stuffy to use quotation marks. Clearly, all you highly literate readers will know that "a consummation devoutly to be wished," which shows up on page 178, or "to the manner born," used nowhere except right here, didn't originate with me!

Writing a book on writing presents special problems. You readers know, of course, that everyone (*except* you, of course) who reads such a book takes fiendish delight in shooting down the writer for any malfeasance. This book should thus give joy to many a heart, in ways this writer shall discover when it is too late.

But no—what I refer to here is the problem of who gets the credit line when a term must be defined—for example, *noun, pronoun,* etc. Most of us first encounter these terms in grade school. If any single individual deserves a tip of the hat here, it is probably the late Frank Colby. He used to write a scholarly and witty column on usage back in the days I was first learning my trade. I have not knowingly stolen any of his definitions, but I have certainly borrowed his approach. He was deeply concerned with defining in plain, nontechnical terms. So am I.

Thanks to books and authors...

The debt this writer owes to the works of Rudolph Flesch, Robert Gunning, H.W. Fowler, Walter B. Pitkin, and Bergen Evans should be obvious. Less obvious, perhaps, is the influence of some others, including Jack Woodford, Theodore Bernstein, Wilson Follett, Robert Graves, Alan Hodge, Isaac Asimov, and Dr. James Boren.

Thanks for permission...

Thanks and appreciation for the use of copyright material: to Bill Gold and *The Washington Post* for permission to use excerpts from "The District Line" column; to William and Mary Morris and Harper and Row, Publishers, Inc., for permission to use excerpts from *The Harper Dictionary of Contemporary Usage;* to John Kidner and Acropolis Books Limited for permission to use quotations from *The Kidner Report,* and to Colman McCarthy and Acropolis Books Limited for permission to use quotations from *Inner Companions.* Finally, special thanks to former Chairman A. Daniel O'Neal and his staff at the Interstate Commerce Commission for permission to reprint portions of his memo (written during his tenure in 1978) entitled "English—Let's use it at the I.C.C."

Thanks to mentors...

With all respect to those listed above, much of what this book preaches does not come out of other books. It stems in large measure from the teachings of a few mentors. First on this list come James R. Aswell and Mazie (Rodgers) Worcester, whom I told you about in the preface. I did not think to mention the next three "master teachers" in earlier editions, but in retrospect I should have. They were all very important influences in my life. So, belatedly, my thanks to—

Miss Martha Shea, who taught English Comp I at my alma mater, Southeast Missouri State College (now Southeast Missouri State University), Cape Girardeau, Missouri. Miss Shea was a phenomenon—an emeritus member of the faculty, well into her seventies, when I took her course. Her influence probably explains why I use more commas than people do nowadays. (Of course, I use more parentheses and dashes than most, too. That's not Martha Shea's fault. She used to give me hell for it—in a most ladylike way.)

Dr. H.O. Grauel, who required his students at Cape to write daily compositions on his special $4'' \times 6''$ cards of his own design—his famous "Grauel Cards." He taught us how important it was—and is—to be concise, even when we used both sides of a card!

Miss Helen Cleaver, an inspiring teacher of French and Spanish who gave me valuable insights into the Romance roots of English.

Thanks to colleagues...

We can learn from our peers. I owe most of all to my friend and colleague who used to sit at the desk next to mine at NASA—Virgil Carrington "Pat" Jones. It was largely at his urging that this book was written. He has blue-penciled the manuscript at several stages—probably not harshly enough, because he is one of the last of the true gentlemen of this world. I accepted many of the changes he recommended, and if I had good sense I would probably have taken the rest.

Special thanks are due also to:

My wife, Poggy, for help with the manuscript, library research, and (at least most of the time) a tolerant attitude.

Lou Hampton, my former partner, who prepared the additional exercises for earlier editions of this book.

John McJennett, editor-writer and information specialist, Department of State and NASA (where we shared an office as fellow speech-writers for a couple of years).

Linda McJ. Micheli, PhD, poet and instructor in writing at Harvard.

Charles E. (Chuck) Waterman, my partner in Speak/Write Systems, Inc. Chuck is a multi-talented writer, public speaker, and communication consultant. He has designed a number of innovative special exercises for this new (fourth) edition of WWP.

Carl Sieg, management specialist and seminar leader.

Lillian Levy, NASA's Senior Science Writer, who first encouraged me to teach seminars in effective writing.

Ralph Gibson, Randolph Hawthorne, and Miles Waggoner, all of NASA's Office of Public Affairs, and all former colleagues.

Dorothy Bernd Williams, writer-editor and seminar leader, Vicore, Inc.

Thanks to the Writer's Center...

This book may be a "first" for a commercially published book, in that I set the type for it myself. If you don't like the typesetting, I'll blame it on the writer's messy manuscript. If you don't like the book, I'll blame it on the amateur typesetter. The work was done on a Compugraphic IV at The Writer's Center, Glen Echo Park, Md., my home away from home. Special thanks to the Director of the Center, Allan Lefcowitz, PhD. My chief regret is that I didn't give Al an earlier look at the manuscript. Even so, I have particularly valued his criticisms and helpful suggestions. I had known him for months before I found out that he is, among other things, a professor of English at the U.S. Naval Academy, a playwright, and the author of *The Prentice-Hall Writer's Handbook,* a standard college text in English composition and rhetoric.

Thanks also to other Writer's Center staff members, particularly Jane Fox, Mary MacArthur, and Kevin Osborn for his suggestions on book design.

And to Acropolis Books Limited...

Special thanks to Margaret Lenzner for editorial and design suggestions, and to Barbara Glaser and Sandy Alpert for their editorial pencils. Last but not least to my most patient of publishers—Al Hackl.

PART ONE

WRITING WITH
PRECISION

The most dangerous illusion that a good writing course will try to shatter is that creative writing is teachable. Writing is; creating isn't. The most a writing course can do is expose the future writer to rules, techniques, habits, styles, and ideas that make it easier to be taught by oneself, not by another, how to create.

—*Colman McCarthy*

1: Introduction

Can good writing be taught?

That depends on what kind of writing you mean.

If you're talking about "creative writing," whatever that is, the answer is an emphatic NO. (And that is the kind of writing Colman McCarthy is talking about in the paragraph quoted above.) Admired literary figures such as James Joyce, Willa Cather, Ernest Hemingway, and John Steinbeck did not learn to write the way they did by listening to learned professors or participating in classroom discussions. Their kind of writing (for simplicity, let's call it "creative" writing) does not come out of academic exercises or textbooks on composition and rhetoric. First of all, a creative writer must have talent: that is the basic ingredient. Undoubtedly, even a born literary genius can and does polish and improve that basic gift, but no creative writer is worthy of being called by that name unless the talent is there to start with.

BUT if you are talking about writing as a craft rather than writing as an art, that's another story. If you are concerned with what we might describe as "practical" or "useful" writing — writing that is clear, precise, well-organized, easy to read and understand — the answer to your question is YES.

The skills and crafts of useful, practical writing can be taught — and learned. Rest assured, however, that acquiring those skills takes plenty of hard work and continuing application. Writing — any kind of writing — isn't easy. And writing that communicates clearly and precisely is usually very hard work indeed. It requires turning on the brain, and very few of us enjoy doing that.

Well-crafted writing, whether literary or useful, can be beautiful. Some lucky individuals can write what my friend Miles Waggoner would call a "singing line." (Miles knows, because he can write that kind of line himself.) Others may work hard for a lifetime and never achieve it, or if they upon occasion do, it is only by accident.

But many of the rest of us, by diligent study and practice, can learn to put together a respectable English sentence. That in itself is no mean feat.

This book is concerned with "useful" writing only: communicating ideas as clearly and crisply — as precisely, if you will — as possible. Doing that is a never-ending and often thankless task. It requires our continuing attention; we tend to grow lazy and to fall into slovenly habits if we do not keep our minds constantly on the job.

What is good useful writing?

Writing is an extremely subjective study in many ways. You and I may not admire or appreciate the same kinds of writing — chances are we often don't — yet we both may be confident our own opinions are best. Quality in anything, after all, is an intangible. A writer whose talent I admire — Robert M. Pirsig — filled page after page in an endeavor to define "Quality." He generated many thought-provoking ideas, but didn't succeed in defining "Quality" — certainly, not to his own satisfaction. (Read *Zen and the Art of Motorcycle Maintenance* anyway. It's an astonishing book.)

How, then, are we going to decide what good writing is, let alone, how are we going to accomplish it?

Surprisingly, the decision is not so difficult as it might at first appear. Sample the comments of some of the recognized experts and you'll find much more of a consensus than you might suppose.

Surprising? Not really. What is perhaps much more surprising is that you, the readers of this book, already have a sound conception of what constitutes clear, *useful* writing, even though you've not given the matter much thought since you were in school.

What makes me think so? For nearly 25 years I have been asking the people I meet — office workers, students, editors, professional writers — even the ubiquitous "man in the street" — the same questions. It no longer seems surprising to find that they all respond with essentially the same answers.

Time after time I have asked, "What are some of the basic elements you believe are important to good, clear, useful writing? What makes such writing different from poor or imprecise writing that is hard (or impossible) to understand? Can you give me some 'rules'?"

The answers, not arranged here in any particular order of importance, inevitably go something like this:

- Be concise. Keep sentences and paragraphs short.
- State your purpose clearly.
- Get straight to the point.
- Be specific; avoid abstractions.
- Know your audience.
- Write to be understood, not to impress.
- Prefer the active voice. Put action in your verbs.
- Weed out unnecessary words, phrases, and ideas.

And so on. Before you go on reading, try this experiment. Ask some of your friends and associates to give you some "rules for clear writing." I'll wager they respond with essentially this same kind of list, with more variations in form than in content.

But, you might ask, if people already know all this, why don't they practice what they preach? (You don't have to look beyond the correspondence on your own desk to discover that they — and you — don't.) Why don't they? And why don't you? Two very good questions. Most of the rest of this book will be devoted to answering them.

Why the confusion about "good usage"?

Is there such a thing as "good usage" or "correct usage" any more? If you've done much reading on the subject, you may wonder. This in spite of the fact that the experts in conventional or traditional grammar are in almost total agreement. What seems to be the problem?

Well, traditional or conventional grammar has been under a concerted attack for some time — from the influential group of scholars known as structural linguists. When you or I hear or read statements made by members of this important branch of linguistic science we must listen with respect — even when we encounter theories that seem very far out to us. For example, "A native speaker of a language cannot make a mistake." That statement is one I've encountered many times;

possibly you've heard it too. No wonder we're confused. Either the statement is ridiculous, or there is no such thing as "correct usage" any more. Right?

Wrong. On the one hand, we cannot afford to dismiss the opinions of the erudite scholars who preach the gospel of structural linguistics. On the other hand, plenty of hard evidence shows traditional grammar is not yet totally out the window; it still deeply concerns many persons, including most professional writers and editors.

In trying to sort things out, we must first be aware of one thing — the structural linguists, in making their statements about native speakers of a language, are referring almost entirely to the *spoken language*. (Many of them, apparently, believe that's the *only* language worth caring about. That's what raises my blood pressure!)

I can assure them — and you — that a great many people care very much about style and usage in the *written language*. And despite all the potshots taken at traditional grammarians, one fact is clear: the language of business, the language of government, the language in which our country's vital communications are conducted — all these are concerned with the supposedly "old-fashioned" or "outmoded" rules of traditional grammar and usage.

Still, the prime concern of this handbook is not with formal grammar. There are plenty of excellent textbooks on that subject already available. No. What is important here is that you, the reader, learn to look at the writing and editing processes in a new and systematic way. As you learn, you'll begin to apply easy and logical principles that will immediately sharpen your writing. *Writing with Precision* is more than the name of this book — it's a goal you can shoot for, every time you have to write.

Why bother to write better?

Most business and government executives, when cornered, will tell you writing is probably the most important single skill an ambitious young person can have. The ability to write well is rare; a person who develops the skill is likely to rise rapidly, so long as the talent doesn't threaten the boss and other powers that be.

People who hate to write, or are afraid to try, often attempt to get by with talk instead. Sometimes this works. Other times (more often than not) it stirs up extra problems and wastes time, money, and energy. Why? Because without the discipline of writing, their spoken efforts often come out half-baked — ill-conceived and ill-expressed.

Writing helps you think.

Communications breakdowns — or worse yet, total lack of communications — are probably the greatest causes of problems in both government and business. The moral is simple: learn to write as crisply and clearly and effectively as you possibly can. Learn to say what you mean and mean what you say.

The economics of clear writing

There are many other good reasons for learning to write better. One of the most important is simple economics.

Do you have any idea what it costs the average organization or agency to turn out a single one-page letter or memo? Take a guess.

If you guessed anything under $7.00, you're living in the past. The latest figures indicate that the cost per typewritten page usually runs between $7.00 and $12.00, depending on various factors including the amount of research involved, and the number of management levels that have to "sign off" on the correspondence.

The computation includes (a) the time it takes an executive to figure out the problem, do any necessary research, and dictate the letter or write a rough draft; (b) the time necessary for the secretary or typist to transcribe, type, and proof. And that's the short, simple version.

In many organizations that would be only the beginning. The letter or memo was probably written by an underling for someone at a higher level to sign. Add the time of an executive in the next echelon. . . and perhaps of another one a notch higher than that. . . and so on, ad infinitum. Now suppose that all of these worthies manage to insert a few editorial changes of their own. I'll bet you know plenty who would feel they aren't earning their pay if they don't mark things up enough to advertise their own expertise. Of course, even a minor change calls for a fresh typing. The overall cost can accelerate like a rocket.

Even though many offices are now equipped with word processing equipment such as Magcard typewriters, the time saved in multiple retypings is not nearly so much as you probably imagine. The main advantage of such equipment is fewer errors — mind you, I'm not knocking that! — and quicker revisions. (But then don't forget to add the monthly cost of your fancy machines to the overhead.)

All right, does it sound hopeless? How are we going to cut down the costs per letter before we all (government *and* industry) go broke?

What if you could reduce the average length of each memo or letter your office turns out — by, say, about 25 percent. Think about it.

What if, simultaneously, you could reduce the time required to write each memo or letter by about that same percentage — or more? Think about that, too.

Because . . . if you follow the principles outlined in this handbook, you're going to achieve those results — time after time, day after day, from here on out to the golden days of retirement.

That's still only the beginning. There's more, lots more.

How much time will your readers save if they can understand the communication the first time they read it instead of the second or the third or the tenth try?

What if you are writing a regulation or an order that must be read by hundreds or thousands or millions of readers instead of just one. Think about all the potential savings in *their* work hours. Finally, consider how great it would be if each one of those umpteen readers would no longer find it necessary to write you letters of inquiry (each of which is also costing somebody from $7.00 to $12.00 to ask what in the world you really meant.

Maybe your company would have enough money left over to give you a big Christmas bonus. Or maybe the government could cut a few taxes.

Okay, maybe we're all dreamers. Still, it *could* happen.

I hope the point is clear. Writing that does not communicate effectively, CONcisely, and PREcisely is costly to both your own organization and to any person(s) or organizations(s) doing business with you.

The life you save . . .

So far, everything I've said on this subject involves dollar economics — an important factor indeed, but not *the* most important. Over the years, many of my seminar students have been involved with writing rules and regulations. Some of these can quite literally mean life or death. Poor, ineffective, or ambiguous writing can kill people. We'd better do our best to remedy that situation, pronto.

My own concern with precision came first with the editing of technical reports on complex military weapons; later, that concern intensified when I began trying to translate difficult Air Force regulations and instructions into language that even high school dropouts could read and understand. That was more than 25 years ago, and I've been concerned with precision ever since.

I realize, of course, that many of you readers will not be concerned with matters of life and death. Even so, a bit of precision won't hurt a thing. The same care in writing that saves lives in one instance might save time or money in another. And that ain't bad either.

Getting down to brass tacks

You can't build a house (a brick house, that is), without bricks. Words and sentences are the bricks — the building blocks — of the writing trade. So those basic items of words and sentences are going to be our first concerns.

In the next few chapters, you're going to work with those building blocks and learn how to sharpen your skills. What's more, you're going to concentrate at first on the EDITING process, not the WRITING process. Good editing is far from easy, but you can learn it much quicker than you can learn the far more complex processes of writing.

Equally important, as you train your editing eye, you'll find yourself gaining new insights into the problems and processes of writing and organizing these latter tasks will become increasingly easy as you work through later units. This system has been verified by hundreds of students attending seminars in Effective Administrative Writing at Georgetown University's Continuing Management Education Program and in other seminars sponsored by both government and industry.

Exercise: Brief Autobiography

At this point, take time out and write a brief autobiography — one or two handwritten pages. Write something about yourself, your job, your education, your interests, your family, your hobbies. What do you enjoy reading for pleasure? Have you published anything? If so, what?

Don't be self-conscious. This exercise is intended to give some idea of your present writing style. It may disclose some of the problems you'll need to work on. Even if you are using this book independently, as a self-teaching device, please go ahead and write. You'll find you can analyze it yourself, later, after you've worked through Part I of this handbook.

Copyreading Marks

In the next chapter you will learn some of the skills of the copyreader and editor. Illustrated below are some of the markings and symbols that professionals use. Study and learn them if you haven't already. It takes much less time to indicate by a hieroglyphic what is to be done — use these marks and you won't have to spend nearly so much time spelling out instructions in detail.

Indent for paragraph	*L* or *¶*
Insert letter	...to furnish accom̃odations...
Delete and bridge over deletion	...to better make provision...
Spell out	...the (Pres.) notified Congress...
Abbreviate	...(General) Jones asserted...
Set in numerals	...a draft call of (seventy-nine) men was issued...
Spell out	(500) persons attended...
Transpose letters	...the frist to make the leap...
Transpose words	...was recently awarded the prize...
Capitalize	...on Wilson st...
Make lower case	...J.D. Mine, Professor of Sociology...
Delete letter	...it benefitted millions...
Emphasize quotation marks edited in	...he said, "I won't go."
Emphasize commas edited in	...said he'd never never go.
Emphasize apostrophes edited in	...said, "I'm not going."
Center, as by-line or subheads	]By James Williams[
Emphasize periods edited in	...to be at the Coliseum. field house

No Passion on Earth
No Love or Hate
Is Equal to the Passion to Change
Someone Else's Draft.

— H. G. Wells

2: The Craft of the Editor

Introduction

In this chapter, you'll learn some basics about the mysterious things an editor is supposed to do. Even more important — you'll also learn what an editor is NOT supposed to do. Next come a few tips on revising or self-editing. And finally, some useful checklists to make your editing process more thorough and systematic. With practice, you'll learn to perform these steps almost automatically.

Remember — walk before you run. The editing skills you learn now will mesh quickly with the writing skills that follow.

Duties and responsibilities of the writer: a preview

You won't encounter exercises in the actual writing process until later in this book. Still, we should clear up one thing right now — where to draw the line on the division of responsibilities between writer and editor. Sometimes you'll be called upon to work on one side of the line, sometimes on the other. If you don't know where that invisible but highly important line is, you're doomed to failure in either case.

Always keep in mind that, first of all, *the writer is responsible for the technical content of a piece of writing.* The writer — not the editor — is supposed to be the expert on the subject matter. There are, of course, exceptions. If you happen to be the writer's boss, for example, that puts a different complexion on the relationship. You may assign a project to a subordinate who has less technical knowledge than you do. If so, you have good reason — as well as the privilege of rank — to question the facts presented as well as the manner of presentation.

Next, recognize that *the writer is responsible for identifying the purpose of the writing.* The writer must decide what needs to be said, remembering always that to waste the reader's time is a cardinal sin. The editor should be free to second-guess the writer by suggesting that more — or less — material should be used to convey the message clearly. The editor may also suggest ways of reorganizing the material to improve clarity or readability.

The writer must identify the audience and determine the best way of communicating the intended purpose directly and effectively to that audience. Here again, the editor may second-guess, and should feel free to suggest changes that would show clearcut improvement.

The writer must learn (as you are learning now) *to employ editing skills, developing the ability to look with a cold eye at all those golden words, and to revise, revise, and revise again.* Later in this chapter, we'll discuss how you, as a writer, can edit your own copy effectively.

Finally, as Allan Lefcowitz of Writer's Center reminds me, *the writer must learn to have a professional attitude toward constructive criticism from the editor.* That isn't always easy. You'd be amazed at how much practice I've had at this over the years without ever learning to enjoy it. Apparently, some of my editors simply don't recognize the prerogatives of genius.

Okay, the lines of demarcation have been drawn. Let's get back to the nuts and bolts of the editorial process.

Duties and responsibilities of the editor: a preview

As an editor, your job is to improve the clarity, accuracy, and effectiveness — the *precision*, if you will — of any manuscript lacking any of these qualities. *It is emphatically NOT your responsibility to make changes for the sake of changes, or because of your own personal preferences (or prejudices).*

Furthermore, you must NOT change the original language so that it ends up saying something the writer didn't intend. Any time you alter the intended meaning, you overstep the bounds.

On the other hand, suppose you discover that the writer has said something you have reason to believe is not what was intended. That's quite possible — indeed, it happens far oftener than it should. As an editor, you have a duty to point out the error — as tactfully as you can, but firmly enough to get the message across. CAUTION: Any time you hear someone say "Do anything you like with this copy — I have no pride of authorship," watch out! What the writer is really saying is that there will be a knock-down-and-drag-out fight over every single word you change. *Everyone* has pride of authorship, admitted or not. Writers simply will not sit idly by and let you carve up their brainchildren.

Take confidence from the fact that almost any editor worthy of the name can improve the work of almost any writer, however talented. The reason? A "cold eye." This is especially true when the original writer has drawn information from source material of dubious quality — badly organized, poorly written, or not factual. Some of these faults almost inevitably rub off; a second writer or editor taking a fresh look has the immediate advantage of being one step further removed from the original garbage.

TEAMWORK is the key to a good relationship between writer and editor. Avoid the adversary attitude; even if you use all the tact at your disposal, there still may be times when you find yourself involved in a shouting match. Be aware that you'll win a few and lose a few. The more editing skills you learn, the more battles you'll win.

Here's a checklist of things a good editor should strive to do in going over a manuscript. We'll discuss these items — or at least most of them — separately as we progress through the handbook and exercises. Right now, you should find it helpful to see the items all at once.

DO:

● Make sure the reader is given all necessary information (Who-What-Where-When-Why-How) — in the clearest, most logical and orderly arrangement possible.

● Guard against factual errors; even though you're not the expert, you may know something the writer doesn't know. If you find mistakes and you know they are mistakes, correct them. If you're not sure, call the writer's attention to the problem with a *FLAG*. (See Handbook Section.)

● Correct all errors in grammar, punctuation, and spelling. Pay special attention to names, addresses, and figures. Check definitions and quotations.

● Make sure that all writing conforms to the accepted practices of your organization. (Check with the organization style book, correspondence manual, or other published authority.)

● Watch out for double or ambiguous meanings and unconscious humor. (A touch of humor in itself is great, but not if it's accidental. Sometimes reading aloud will help you detect problems in this area.)

● Put yourself in the intended reader's place — watch the *tone* as well as the meaning. Guard against bad taste, officiousness, or other offensiveness. Read for the *connotation* (emotional overtone) as well as the *denotation* (definition) of words.

● Edit first for clarity and precision of meaning, then for conciseness of expression. But remember that conciseness can be an extremely valuable tool in obtaining the clarity you seek.

● Pay close attention to *format.* Help the reader get a *handle* by using appropriate typographical devices: headings, subheadings, bullets, numbered or lettered listings, italicized words, and indented paragraphs.

● Check "breakdowns" against "summaries." Add all figures to ensure that arithmetic is correct and consistent.

Now for the DON'TS:

● DON'T make changes for the sake of changes.

● DON'T introduce errors of fact under the guise of making the writing easier to read and understand. Easy reading isn't much help if it gives incorrect information.

● DON'T take anything on faith. Be curious — and suspicious. Check out anything that sounds even remotely doubtful.

● DON'T permit overuse of technical *jargon, abbreviations, acronyms,* or other technical shoptalk or shorthand. Remember, although they can save time and space when properly used, they may not be familiar to all readers. If there's a chance some readers won't understand them, urge the writer to spell out the terms (or define them in lay language) the first time they are used.

● DON'T be afraid of showing your ignorance if you're not sure about something. You'll find out the hard way that it's much more embarrassing to let something get by that is wrong. Your readers will inform you of the error of your ways very quickly, and not always gently. So — play it safe. Ask an expert on the subject, particularly if you're working in an unfamiliar area.

You can't expect to remember all these items at first. Don't give up. With practice, they will soon become almost second nature. For the time being, just refer to this checklist and use it systematically, one step at a time. Before long you won't need the list.

The rules of editing

More than a quarter of a century ago, I worked in the pioneering "Effective Writing Program" of the United States Air Force. It was a very educational experience. Our task was to rewrite Air Force regulations, manuals, and other official publications as clearly and precisely as we possibly could.

The writers I was supposed to be directing had their own opinions and ideas about how the job should be done. Diversity and originality are great, but we were getting more variety than the Chief of Staff really wanted. So we began to hold staff meetings to pull together the best ideas into a uniform approach. Those meetings evolved into my effective writing seminars — and after many years, this book.

As I have said, we were concerned with accuracy and precision above all else. Our First Commandment was to make official Air Force publications easier to read and understand *without changing their meanings.* The legal staff was constantly looking over our shoulders to make sure we didn't.

We mutually agreed that neither writing nor law can ever be an exact science. But we also agreed that you have to hang in there and try. As we compared notes, we began to detect patterns. We read the works of the pioneers of the field — Rudolph Flesch, Robert Gunning, Walter Pitkin, and others. We "borrowed" or adapted ideas that worked, and added ideas of our own. Eventually came the happy discovery that a few relatively simple "rules" would solve the great majority of the common difficulties.

The "rules" were, of course, not actually rules at all. There is nothing "official" about them. They haven't been handed down on tablets of stone. You may find that sometimes by breaking one or all of them, you may actually improve a given piece of writing.

Because we are concerned with using the right word instead of the almost right word, let's replace "rules" with "principles." That is what they really are. But whatever you call them, please learn them and apply them before you decide to break them!

I have revised and reorganized the list many times over the years, on the basis of continuing experience. This is the latest version. I am listing them in summary form here; I'll elaborate and explain each one in detail.

Ten principles for improving clarity and precision of written documents

1. Prefer the active voice.
2. Don't make nouns out of good, strong "working verbs."
3. Be concise. Cut out all excess baggage. Keep your *average* sentence length under 20 words.
4. Be specific. Use concrete terms instead of generalizations.
5. Keep related sentence elements together; keep unrelated elements apart. Place modifiers as close as possible to the words they are intended to modify.
6. Avoid unnecessary shifts of *number, tense, subject, voice,* or *point of view.*
7. Prefer the simple word to the farfetched, and the right word to the almost right.
8. Don't repeat words, phrases, or ideas needlessly. But don't hesitate to repeat when the repetition will increase clarity.
9. Use *parallelism* whenever it is appropriate — that is, when you are expressing similar thoughts, make sure you write your sentences so that the elements are in similar or parallel form. But *do not* use parallel structure when expressing thoughts that are not truly similar.
10. Arrange your material logically. Always begin with ideas the reader can readily understand. If you must present difficult material, go *one step at a time.* Do not skip any steps. Arrange your format to give the reader every possible "handle" on the material.

Study and use these ten principles until they become second nature. Even if — Heaven forbid — you learn nothing else about grammar or style, these simple principles alone will eliminate most of the common errors of business writing. (NOTE: Some of the grammatical or technical terms used in this chapter may not be familiar to you. You'll find definitions of these terms in the Handbook section.)

How to edit your own copy — the hardest editorial task of all

Why is it so hard to edit your own copy?

Mostly, because you're so familiar with the ideas you are expressing that you may think you've stated them quite clearly when actually you have not. That's why a "cooling off" period is so important any time you aren't facing a tight deadline.

If possible, put your manuscript away when you finish it; work on a totally unrelated project. Keep your golden words in your hold basket or a bottom drawer for at least three days. By then they won't look quite so golden. You'll be able to spot problems you otherwise would have missed. And remember — even a brief cooling off is better than none.

The next suggestion may seem far out — particularly if you don't intend to become a professional writer or editor. On the other hand, many of my seminar students have told me they have learned to enjoy this little game.

Have I created enough mystery? The tip is this: practice reading *everything* you come across — every bit of correspondence, every memo or report, even your daily newspaper — with a stern and critical editorial eye. Does that sound dull? Not really. It can be fun. Almost every day you'll find choice little items such as this one — a caption that appeared beneath a picture on the sports page of the *Washington Star-News,* 12 June 1976:

> Pele, the star of Team America, soothes the ankle he sprained in a scrimmage with an ice pack.

Editorial comment: You had better watch out for those fierce ice packs.

Or how about this one? Turnabout is fair play, so we'll quote a few lines from the *Washington Post.* Here's the first sentence of a movie review that appeared on 13 June 1976. Please note that the whole paragraph is just one sentence:

> The film-making husband-and-wife team of Volker Schlondorff and Margarethe von Trotta won quite a few admirers with "A Free Woman," but they should add quite a few thousand more with this compelling and thought-provoking adaptation of Nobel Prizewinner Heinrich Boll's 1974 novel about the grimly ironic repercussions of a case of character assassination by newspaper, inspired by the writer's own clashes with the peculiarly virulent and vindictive right-wing yellow press of West Germany.

Get the idea? Once you start looking, you can turn up gems such as these almost every day. In the process, you'll become more alert to the differences between good and bad, clear and unclear writing. Learning to recognize the differences will speed you along in the difficult process of becoming a better editor.

With practice, you'll soon learn the basic editing steps most professionals use. At first you'll proceed one step at a time, very systematically. Later, as your skills improve, you'll combine several or all steps in a single pass.

Checklist: steps in revising or self-editing

Here is a brief checklist you can use as a reminder when editing your own copy:

1. Read all the way through your manuscript — or a unit of it, such as a section or a chapter — before you begin to make *any* editorial changes. Make sure you get the total picture. Ask the questions a newspaper reporter would ask: Who-What-When-Where-How-Why, not necessarily in that exact order. Then carefully check to make sure you haven't omitted any of these essential facts.

2. Read through again; now begin to apply the principles described earlier in this chapter. If you find it easier to do so, take one principle at a time. That may seem slow at first, but as you get the hang of it, the process will go much faster. Pay special attention to getting rid of passive constructions and smothered verbs. You'll be surprised how this will sharpen and strengthen your writing.

3. Boil down sentences by making one word replace several words or a phrase. Cut the deadwood and *redundancy.* Keep the *average* sentence length under 20 words if you can. Remember, fewer words than that will usually be even better.

4. Re-read your manuscript one more time, *aloud.* The ear can detect flaws the eye misses. Check for logic and completeness; search for "wrong words" that are inappropriately used or have undesirable *connotations.* Put yourself in the reader's shoes and see if the writing tells the things he or she would want and need to know. If necessary, add an *example,* a *definition,* or an *analogy.*

*The chief aim of the writer
is to be understood.*

*—John Dryden, 17th Century
essayist*

3: Editing for Strength

Introduction

Administrative writing is loaded with *passive constructions,* and I do mean loaded. Why?

Habit, mostly. Nobody has ever pinpointed where or when it happened, but the evidence is clear: somebody who had the power to do so must have laid down the law —Administrative writing must be impersonal and indirect. Since that evil day, the style has caught on better than hula hoops or skateboards ever did. Passive constructions have multiplied faster than bunny rabbits.

But perhaps I'm getting ahead of myself. Let's begin at the beginning, which I should have done in the first place. You, the reader, have every right to be asking, "What in the world *is* a passive construction, anyway?"

Some of you undoubtedly do remember the distinction between *active* and *passive voice.* Others probably haven't thought much about formal grammar or definitions for a long time — perhaps not since grade school or high school days. So I hope the rememberers will forgive me for refreshing the memories of the forgetters.

Definitions of **active** and **passive voice**

When a sentence is written in the *active voice,* the subject performs the action. When a sentence is written in the *passive voice,* the subject is acted upon.

For example, *I rang the bell* is in the active voice. *The bell was rung by me* is in the passive voice. Again, *This office completed the action* is in the active voice; *The action was completed by this office* is in the passive voice.

As you can see by these examples, the *active voice* gives writing a sense of strength, energy, vitality, and motion. The *passive voice* slows things down.

Look hard at the memos and letters crossing your desk; see how many passive constructions you can spot. You'll probably be surprised. In government and business writing, one fault stands out: *overuse of the passive voice is by far the biggest single offense.*

Most of the "experts" — Strunk and White, Gunning, Flesch, and all the rest, warn us against passives. But they put this particular "rule" well down the list. In my book (that's a pun, son) it comes up as Rule Number One. Nothing else you can learn will do so much, so quickly, to improve conciseness, readability, and precision.

Try it for yourself. Go through a piece of writing looking for passives; then rewrite the sentences using active constructions. Not only will the revised version be stronger and straighter, but *it will be 20 to 30 percent shorter as well.*

This phenomenon, incidentally, is the strongest argument you have *for convincing management it's time for a change.* Obviously, any device that can cut average sentence length by roughly a third — and that's what changing passives to actives can do — is worth using.

Make every word count

We have said earlier, and now shamelessly repeat, that clear writing is *concise.* That doesn't mean quite the same thing as *short;* to be *concise* means, in a nutshell, that you *make every word count,* and eliminate all extraneous material.

Structural linguists (see, I quote them joyfully when what they say suits my purpose!) have found that in general writing, about 75 percent of all sentences follow the basic subject-verb-object (S-V-O) pattern. But, they tell us, *in official writings — both government and industry —*

about 75 percent or more of the sentences are written indirectly. That is, the word that should be the *object* becomes the *subject.*

I know you're getting weary of hearing it. I'm weary of saying it. But it must be said: *There seems to be an unwritten rule that everything must be stated in the passive voice.* And that's what it is — an *unwritten* rule. Nowhere has any management ever spelled out any such rule. So, for Heaven's sake, let's wipe it out here and now. It's a bummer.

Passive constructions are bad enough any time, but they're worst of all when used in directives, instructions, or regulations. Suppose an organization posts a rule for its employees: *A copy of each sales letter originated in Division A will be submitted to the vice president in charge of sales.*

That sounds simple enough. But — is it likely to get the job done? Will the copies be submitted as ordered?

Perhaps they will. But then again, perhaps they won't. Who is actually responsible for carrying out the order? The trouble with this kind of passive construction is that it leaves out the key point — *who is supposed to do the work?*

Wouldn't it be better to say: *The sales manager for Division A must send the vice president in charge of sales a copy of each sales letter originated in the division.* (We know that the sales manager's secretary will probably do the actual sending — but we also know that the *responsibility* for the job has now been nailed down.)

Let's consider another example. Suppose we write something like *This regulation will be explained to each new employee.* Who's supposed to do the explaining? The reader has to guess. Let's write, instead, *The branch chief will explain this regulation to each new employee.*

Perhaps I should mention that *technical editing* offers some slightly different problems. In that field you'll find passives being used constantly. The reason for using the passive in such writing makes a bit more sense: namely, to keep the personal element out of the writing. Here's a typical example:

After the frammis is unscrewed from the dohickey, it should be thoroughly washed in solvent and inspected for cracks in the surface; then the threads should be checked before it is reinserted in the dohickey.

Still, wouldn't it be clearer to write:

(a) Unscrew the frammis from the dohickey; (b) wash it thoroughly in solvent; (c) inspect it for cracks in the surface; (d) make sure the threads are clean and not stripped; and (e) reinsert the frammis in the dohickey.

Principle One:

PREFER
THE
ACTIVE VOICE

Principle Two:

Don't make
NOUNS
out of
good
strong,
working
VERBS

Most readers can follow this kind of instruction quite easily. The results will usually be much better than those achieved in following a straight narrative version of the same information. So, think twice before you buy the old "technical writing" excuse for using passives. Sometimes, maybe. All the time? No way.

When should you use a passive construction?

Does all this mean that the active voice is preferable to the passive voice *every time?*

Not at all. The passive exists for a reason. Sometimes you may be very glad it's available. It can be quite useful upon occasion.

For example, you should use a *passive construction* when the performer of the action is unknown or irrelevant. You can use passives to advantage, also, when the emphasis is (a) on the receiver of the action; (b) on the verb; or (c) even on the modifier.

Here's the rule of thumb I use in my own writing to ascertain whether an active or a passive construction would be preferable:

If the person or thing receiving the action is more important than the person or thing doing the action, use the passive.

If the person or thing doing the action is unknown or unimportant, use the passive.

For example, it would probably be better to use the passive in a sentence like this one: *The Senator was struck by a golf ball.* The active-voice version, *A golf ball struck the Senator,* is actually a weaker construction in this instance. The key is that, after all, the Senator (or at least, we hope *most* Senators) can be considered to be more important than most golf balls.

All this lengthy dissertation has been leading up to what I consider to be the most important single principle for improving most administrative writing. Here it is in its own box:

PRINCIPLE ONE: Prefer the active voice.

By now you should understand not only why this principle is important, but you should also understand why we use the word "prefer." Remember that there are indeed some cases when the passive voice may be preferable.

What you need now is some actual practice in spotting passives and changing them to actives. Here's a preliminary exercise that starts out very simply, but gets a bit harder as you go along.

Preliminary Exercise: Passive Constructions

Change the passives to actives in the following sentences. Make other minor editorial changes you believe will improve strength or clarity, if you so desire.

1. The letter was written by the manager.
2. The accounts were balanced by a CPA.
3. A duplicate sales slip was furnished by the clerk.
4. A commotion was caused by the children in the front row.
5. An argument was prevented by the referee.
6. The papers were filed by the attorney for the defense.
7. It is requested that this report be submitted by 30 June.
8. A motion was made by John Smith to table the action until Tuesday.
9. The pistol was dropped by the burglar as he fled from the store.
10. The storeroom had been left unlocked by someone.

Did you have any trouble with any of these sentences? You probably did not, but if there are any you aren't sure about, you may find the following suggested rewrites helpful. (In this, as in most of the exercises in this book, you'll find there are seldom any absolutely right or absolutely wrong answers. Sometimes several different answers will be almost equally good or equally poor, with various gradations in between. You will have to learn to develop confidence in your own editorial judgment.)

Suggested Rewrites for Preliminary Exercise: Passive Constructions

1. The manager wrote the letter.
2. A CPA balanced the accounts.
3. The clerk furnished a duplicate sales slip.
4. The children in the front row caused a commotion.
5. The referee prevented an argument.

6. The attorney for the defense filed the papers. (OR, perhaps you decided to make the sentence more concise by changing it to read, "The defense attorney filed the papers." If you did, that's great. You're already ahead of the game.)

7. Please submit this report by 30 June. (Notice that this sentence, and others like it, can be restated crisply and clearly by using what we call in the language of grammar the *imperative mood*. The imperative expresses commands, such as "Do your work; finish your assignment," etc. We'll discuss the imperative further in later chapters. Note also that we keep the concept of a *request* rather than a *command* by using the word "please."

8. John Smith made a motion to table the action until Tuesday. (OR, perhaps you improved the sentence even more by writing, "John Smith *moved* to table the action . . .)

9. The burglar dropped the pistol as he fled from the store.

10. Someone had left the storeroom unlocked. (NOTE: The "had left" — which is the *past perfect* form of the verb — is important. You should not have changed it to the straight *past tense* "left." Remember that you, as an editor, must preserve the same shade of meaning the original writer intended. The past perfect tense indicates that an action or condition was begun in the past and completed in the past, before the other past action or condition.)

You will find other, more difficult exercises at the back of this book. Please don't skip them. They are designed to increase your understanding of the passive voice, how to recognize it, how to change it to the active voice and, on rare occasions, how to use the passive voice effectively when it is preferable to the active voice.

Smothered verbs

When I was studying Freshman English back in the dark ages, one of my professors liked to talk about "controverted verbs" — an academic term for verbs that have been changed or transformed into nouns. Your teacher may call these *smothered verbs,* instead. This term means the same thing, and is a much neater appellation.

The main trouble with smothered verbs is this: any time you change a working verb to a noun, you must add another verb to complete the sentence. (To get back to basics, think of the definition of a sentence that you probably had to memorize back in the third grade: *A sentence is a group of words containing a subject and a predicate and expressing a complete thought.*) Obviously, then, when you smother a working verb, turning it into a noun, you will have to replace it with another verb in order to make a complete sentence. Usually, the word that replaces the working verb will be some form of *to be,* and there won't be any action.

PRINCIPLE TWO: Don't make nouns out of good, strong "working verbs."

What is a *working verb*? One that expresses action. Strong, working verbs are the backbone of English sentence structure. They are the engines that make sentences move; they put action into writing.

Why, then, should anyone want to change useful, hardworking verbs into long-winded nouns, by adding endings such as *-ance, -tion, -ization,* and so on? Frankly, I don't know, but it's a very popular custom in most administrative writing.

Let's consider an example or two:

SMOTHERED: Authorization for the absence was given by the leader.
IMPROVED: The leader authorized the absence.

You can see from this example that smothered verbs and passive constructions frequently go together. In fact, they are almost inseparable. If you can unsmother a verb and, at the same time, change a passive to an active construction, you'll cut sentence length by a third.

SMOTHERED: My new assistant is negligent in the details of his work.
IMPROVED: My new assistant neglects the details of his work.

It is also possible to derive *adjectives* from verbs. You can probably think of many words that have both a noun and a verb form, or an adjective and a verb form. Think hard and you may come up with some that have all three forms — verb, adjective, and noun. Sometimes a word may have exactly the same form as a noun and as a verb — for example, *answer, end, estimate, index,* and *reply.* Be aware of this, but don't worry about it. All you need to remember is that many problems that plague administrative writers stem from overuse of smothered verbs with endings such as *ion, -tion, -ment, -ance, -ancy,* and *-ization.*

In the box just below is a simple preliminary exercise you can use for a warmup.

Preliminary Exercise: Smothered Verbs

Write the root verbs of the following:

1. authorization
2. performance
3. illustration
4. implementation
5. advancement
6. realization
7. transmittal
8. confrontation
9. documentation
10. negotiation
11. concession
12. quotation
13. employment
14. determination
15. relation
16. administration

You shouldn't have had any trouble with these, but if you have any doubts, here's a checklist: (1) authorize; (2) perform; (3) illustrate; (4) implement; (5) advance; (6) realize; (7) transmit; (8) confront; (9) document; (10) negotiate; (11) concede; (12) quote; (13) employ; (14) determine; (15) relate; and (16) administer. I hope you didn't lull yourself into saying "confrontate" or "documentate" or "administrate." If that happened, cheer up. You're not the first.

You'll find an additional exercise on page 193 in Part Three of the book. Don't skip it.

If it is possible to cut a word out, always cut it out.

— *George Orwell,* Essay on "Politics and the English Language"

4: Editing for Conciseness and Clarity

Introduction

Most administrative writing contains a high percentage of unnecessary words and phrases. A skillful editor can often cut a manuscript by half, simply through pruning the deadwood.

Here's a typical example:

BEFORE: This is in reference to your letter of 28 April, in which you requested further information about the status of your application and also queried as to whether or not it will be necessary for you to furnish additional references and supporting documents.

AFTER: We can finish processing your application as soon as you send us a certified copy of your military discharge certificate. That's all we need.

Note that the "Before" version contains 43 words, and hasn't even started. The reader is being told things already known, and the answers to the questions will require still more words. The "After" version contains 24 words, answers both of the reader's questions, and requires no preliminaries.

The situation is somewhat different if you are answering, say, an inquiry from a Senator, whose office turns out dozens or even hundreds of letters every day. You will help the Senator's staff (let's be realistic) figure out which letter (and which constituent) is involved by referring to the date and subject. But that's a different ballgame. In most letters to the general public, it is totally unnecessary to repeat what is said in a letter to which you are responding. (The private individual doesn't write all that many letters.) Just be sure to phrase your answers in a way that will help recall the questions without the need for repeating them.

Why is conciseness so important?

Numerous scientific and psychological studies show that long sentences are harder to understand than short ones. (Like many other scientific truths, this one seems much too obvious for all the bother about it.) You can easily check this out for yourself. Turn back to page 17 and read the one-sentence paragraph there. Time yourself. Now see how much of it you can remember. Fair enough?

When you have finished, try this mildly edited version the same way:

> The film-making husband-and-wife team of Volker Schlondorff and Margarethe von Trotta won quite a few admirers with "A Free Woman." They should, however, add quite a few thousand more with this compelling and thought-provoking adaptation of Nobel Prize-winner Heinrich Boll's 1974 novel. The book concerns the grimly ironic repercussions of a case of character assassination by newspaper; it was inspired by the writer's own clashes with the peculiarly virulent and vindictive right-wing yellow press of West Germany.

By dividing this passage up into bite-sized ideas, this very simple editing makes life much easier for the reader. One of my early idols, the late Walter Pitkin, once wrote that a sentence " . . . grows worse by the square of the number of words it contains, to put it very roughly. A poorly built sentence of twenty words is about four times as hard to attend to and to understand as an equally poor sentence of ten words." (*The Art of Useful Writing,* pp. 51-52.)

Pitkin's excellent advice about using short sentences has been strongly reinforced by the works of such "readability experts" as Rudolph Flesch and Robert Gunning. They (and many others) advise readers to keep their sentences short and sweet if they want to be read and understood. For a more detailed treatment of this subject, see *Readability Formulas,* listed alphabetically in the Handbook Section of this opus.

You can follow their advice without having to write primer-like prose. Heaven forbid. A long succession of sentences, structured always in the simple declarative, is guaranteed to drive adult readers straight up the wall. You know the kind I mean: *I see the cat. The cat is black. He is a nice cat.* I suspect these sentences don't thrill children all that much either. No wonder they have such a rough time learning to read.

What can the writer do about this? Simple: just balance short sentences with longer ones. Keep the *average* sentence length under 20 words — and fewer words are even better, most of the time, and for most readers.

Proper punctuation helps readers understand long sentences. (And keep in mind that long sentences are okay — *once in a while.*) Good, workmanlike constructions with clearly defined relationships and carefully placed modifiers can make such sentences easy to follow. But — beginners beware. George Bernard Shaw could fashion marvelously balanced sentences of 100 words or more. That doesn't mean the rest of us should rush out and try it.

Break some of the really long thoughts into shorter segments. Later, when you are doing *readability tests* or *fog counts,* remember that for such purposes you don't always have to consider the period as the only "full stop." If you break up sentences with *semicolons, dashes, question marks,* and other punctuation marks that indicate a strong pause, that's okay. You don't have to rely on periods every time.

PRINCIPLE THREE: Be concise. Cut out all excess baggage. Keep your average sentence length under 20 words.

As we have seen, long and complicated sentences can make life very difficult for the average reader. Let's look briefly now at some of the underlying problems. Time and space permitting, we could spend many pages on this one subject, but we'll just try for the high points. Here are a few common difficulties to watch out for:

Redundancy

In the space program, "redundant" was a good word. In writing, it's a bad one. Space engineers borrowed the term, but in their parlance, a *redundant* component is a back-up to another used for the same purpose. It's designed to build in extra safety, and we can't fault that.

In space, it isn't so easy to go back for a spare part.

In writing, on the other hand, you almost never need a back-up. Say a thing one time, clearly, and that should be ample. The reader, at least figuratively, can go back — re-reading, even several times, if necessary. So you, the writer, needn't waste words.

There are, as always, a few exceptions. In a long piece of writing, put a summary at the end, reiterating important points. This ensures that your reader will remember them, and saves time in the process.

To be concise, don't repeat words or ideas unnecessarily. Also, don't give both the positive and negative of an idea if one of them alone would suffice for understanding.

Suppose, for example, we have a statement to this effect:

> It would appear that proper planning, coordination, and execution of the project, if achieved, will permit the building to be finished on time and within budget.

Now, continuing, this positive statement is followed by a negative:

> However, we recognize that any failure during one or more of these important preliminary steps will undoubtedly result in a failure to meet the completion schedule and/or the likelihood of bringing in the project at higher costs than had been initially envisioned.

Why state this both ways? To save words, use one statement or the other, not both. And preferably, as Johnny Mercer put it, "Accentuate the positive."

Wordiness

"Wordiness" is not the same thing as redundancy, but it's a first cousin. Wordy writing is caused by using more words than you need to express an idea. Watch out particularly for needless repetitions of the same word or words in a sentence or paragraph. For example:

> WORDY: Company health records are further subdivided into two sections which are medical treatment records and dental treatment records. Medical treatment records will be contained in Form 20-A. Dental treatment records will be contained in Form 20-B.

Here's a suggested rewrite:

> Company health records are further subdivided in Medical Treatment Records (Form 20-A) and Dental Treatment Records (Form 20-B).

Conceivably, we could have cut another "records" or two, but perhaps at the loss of some clarity. So, don't repeat words unnecessarily, but don't be afraid to repeat if you think the reader will understand more clearly. Okay?

Sometimes the difference between redundancy and wordiness is not so clear. The following example to some extent illustrates a combination of the two:

> This regulation prescribes uniform policies and procedures by which servicing from the Department of the Air Force to the Department of the Navy may be effected in support of Military Air Transportation System (MATS) aircraft and personnel assigned by the Department of the Navy, and from the Department of the Navy to the Department of the Air Force in support of MATS aircraft and personnel assigned by the Department of the Air Force. This regulation applies to Air Force and Navy installations and activities in the Zone of the Interior and overseas.

Try your hand at rewriting. Then you can compare your version with the way we rewrote the paragraph in the Air Force "Effective Writing Program" more than 25 years ago. Maybe your version will be better.

> This regulation tells how the Department of the Air Force and the Department of the Navy can give reciprocal service to Military Air Transportation System (MATS) aircraft and personnel assigned by the other Department. This regulation applies to all Air Force and Navy installations and activities world wide.

Words with overlapping meanings

Another common fault in administrative writing stems from a bad habit that afflicts many of us. The words of certain trite phrases seem locked together in our minds; we carelessly use these words in the same combinations time after time. What's worse, we often pile up several of these offenders in the same sentence. One such expression leads to another, unless we stay constantly alert. Here are some typical examples. Keep a sharp lookout for them.

DON'T SAY	SAY
absolutely complete	complete
advance planning	planning
ask the question	ask
assembled together	assembled

continue on	continue
cooperate together	cooperate
consensus of opinion	consensus
each and every	each *or* every, not both
enclosed herewith	enclosed
exactly identical	identical
expired and terminated	expired *or* terminated, not both
repeat again	repeat
same identical	same
still remains	remains
the reason is because	because

Roundabout prepositional phrases

We have said that unnecessary words in a sentence stand between you and your reader. Some of the worst offenders are longwinded prepositional phrases. Many times you can cut down on them sharply by referring to this list.

LONGWINDED	STRAIGHTFORWARD
along the lines of	like
as of this date	today
as to	about (or leave out entirely)
at the present time	now
by means of	with, by
for the purpose of	for
for the reason that	since, because
from the point of view of	for
inasmuch as	for, as
in order to	to
in a position to	can, may
in the possession of	has, have
in a satisfactory manner	satisfactorily
in the case of	if
in view of	because, since
in the nature of	like
in the event of	if
in connection with	of, in, on
in relation to	toward, to

in the amount of	for
in a number of cases	some
on the basis of	by
on the grounds that	since, because
owing to the fact that	since, because
on the part of	by, among, for
on behalf of	for
on a few occasions	occasionally
prior to	before
subsequent to	after
with a view to	to
with reference to	about (or leave out)
with regard to	about (or leave out)
with the result that	so that

By all this I don't mean to imply that you should *never* use any of the phrases listed in the left column. Sometimes they can be quite useful. Make a considered judgment: if you then decide such a phrase or phrases will add needed emphasis, or give your sentence a better cadence, use it. But keep on guard. Don't use any of them *habitually*.

Preliminary Exercise: Conciseness

Strike out all the wasted or unnecessary words in the following sentences. Feel free to rewrite the sentences completely if you believe that further changes will clarify meaning.

1. They all arrived at a consensus of opinion in regard to the basic principle that the continuing utilization of the wornout methodology of the electoral college is antiquated, outdated, and generally inefficient.

2. In very few cases, if any, do members of politically liberal types of groups have any degree of approval concerning the free and totally unrestricted widespread proliferation of unlicensed handguns, pistols, automatics, revolvers, and sidearms.

3. During the time period that the two elderly old gentlemen were patiently waiting for the governor to make his arrival upon the scene, they whiled away the idle hours by participating in the ancient and fascinating game known the world over as chess.

4. During the entire chronological time-frame of reference that Abner Jones was a participating member of the naval portion of America's armed forces, he had the opportunity to participate in only one sea voyage.

5. Because of the unfortunate fact that it happened to be raining at that particular period in time, we came to the conclusion that we would refrain from going to the outdoor concert.

6. By approximately 10:05 o'clock a.m. on the morning of the following day, a rather slight but steady drizzle of rainfall had muddied up the surface of the ground to a considerable extent, and this fortuitous but fortunate occurrence made the tracks of the fugitive readily visible to the unaided eye of the sheriff.

7. The new highrise motel building is constructed of steel, with very large glass window areas from bottom to top. It has a large and very conspicuous neon sign displayed somewhat flamboyantly upon the roof. You can thus identify the building quite plainly even when you are viewing it from quite a considerable distance away.

8. It so happens that there turned out to be a grand total of five persons among the onlookers and spectators who were equipped with flashlights as a part of their emergency paraphernalia.

You will find some suggested answers below. Remember, there is no single "right" or "wrong" way to edit any of these sentences. Your own versions might be better.

Suggested Answers to Preliminary Exercise: Conciseness

1. All agreed that the electoral college is outdated and inefficient. (Perhaps you used "They" instead of "All." Not bad, but you lost the idea of unanimity implied by the "all" in the original version. (We could argue about it, but let's not.)

2. Liberals seldom approve of unlicensed handguns.

3. Patiently awaiting the governor's arrival, the two old men played chess.

4. While Abner Jones was in the U.S. Navy, he made only one sea voyage. (Perhaps you left out the word "sea." Okay, but don't forget that a few years ago, during the Apollo Program, an all-Navy crew made a "space voyage" to the Moon.)

5. It was raining, so we decided not to go to the outdoor concert.

6. By about 10 o'clock the next morning, a slight but steady drizzle had muddied the ground enough to make the fugitive's tracks easily visible to the sheriff. (Or maybe you said, " . . . easy for the sheriff to see the fugitive's tracks.")

7. The new steel-and-glass highrise motel, with its large and conspicuous neon sign on the roof, can be plainly seen from afar.

8. Five of the spectators had flashlights.

Let's try a harder exercise this time, based on a real document.

Exercise: Conciseness

This is a very difficult exercise. Consider it a challenge! I did not make it up — the following paragraph is an excerpt from a real document. "Only the names have been changed to protect the innocent." Read it through carefully. See if you can understand it on first reading. If you can, you're a better reader than most people.

Take a few moments to analyze why this material is so difficult to understand. Then see if you can rewrite it more clearly. I'll give you a few hints when you are ready to begin.

USE OF FIREARMS BY AGENCY PERSONNEL. In addition to the requirements set forth by the Department concerning the use of firearms, agency personnel covered by this order shall resort to the use of firearms only when there is a clear and present danger of serious injury to/or loss of life of the law enforcement officer or security guard or innocent bystander resulting from a display of deadly force on the part of another individual, and then only to that extent which is necessary to render the individual responsibile for the threat incapable of continuing the activity which prompted the law enforcement officer, security officer or contract guard to use a firearm.

All right, let's look at this together. Note that readers must decipher a sentence more than 100 words long. By any readability scale ever devised, this sentence is monstrous. Still, it's truly no worse than many others I've encountered.

Ask the question, first of all, "Who is supposed to read this regulation and understand it — and, more important, *comply* with it?" (Are the individuals being addressed likely to have more than a high school education?)

Next question: "Is it important that the reader understand every detail?" (You'd better believe it. This regulation carries a grave responsibility: to spell out specifically when to draw, and if necessary, *fire,* a deadly weapon. Human lives are at stake.)

Next question: "How many different ideas are packed within that one sentence?" Here's a quick summary for you: (a) other (Department) requirements; (b) *who* is covered by the regulation; (c) *what* the personnel concerned are supposed to do; (d) *when* they are supposed to do it; (e) *what other persons* are involved; and (f) *when* the use of firearms is supposed to stop.

Suggestion: take special care to ensure that your rewrite covers all these points. The clearest way to do this would be to discuss each point in a separate sentence, or at least a separate clause.

Probably neither you nor I could come up with a perfect rewrite, even with more information than we're given here. The first step in real life would be to confer with a member of the legal staff. For example, what does "resort to the use of firearms" mean? Does that mean placing a hand on the weapon? Drawing it? Firing it? Frankly, I don't know. I've had police officers tell me they've been instructed not to draw a weapon unless they intend to fire, and not to fire unless they are shooting to kill — UNLESS their intended target is fleeing. The "Code of the West" says it's a sin to shoot people in the back. If all this confuses you, it confuses me, too. But you will undoubtedly run across problems at least this difficult in real life. When that time comes, be sure to do your homework.

Another question: What if there is a 'clear and present danger of serious injury to/or loss of life of' another criminal, rather than an 'innocent bystander'? Should a firearm then be used? (I would think probably not, but it's a question to consider. A conscientious editor would not fail to check out such contingencies.)

And so on. Remember, this is just an exercise; here you're more concerned with word choice and sentence structure than with legal technicalities. The latter are beyond the scope of this book. All I can say is: *Check and doublecheck.*

Too much of a good thing?

Is it possible to be *too* concise?

Indeed it is. Cutting too much can be even worse than cutting too little. If you strip your writing to the barest statement of fact, eliminating every shred of supporting detail, you'll inevitably reduce clarity. What's worse, you'll risk losing the reader's interest as well.

Avoid also any tendency to copy foibles of newspaper style — particularly the recent tendency to omit the articles *a, the,* and *an.* That would be okay for saving words in a telegram — in the olden days, we used to have to fit messages into ten words — but who writes telegrams any more? Still the telegraphic style lingers. I suggest we retire the telegraphese as well as the telegraph itself.

Too much conciseness can also be construed by readers as bad manners, or at best, a lack of concern. If someone has written you a lengthy letter or report — one that clearly reflects thought and effort, you need to respond with more than a simple "okay" pencilled on the buckslip. If you've studied anything about Transactional Analysis, you know that a bit of "stroking" is in order. Even though the answer you have given is a positive one, that in itself is not enough. Take the time to write at least a few lines, even though you *could* convey the message in fewer words. Again, common sense and common courtesy — neither being all that common — should be the guiding principles.

Principle Three:

BE CONCISE

Cut out all excess baggage
Keep your AVERAGE sentence length under 20 words.

I keep six honest serving men
(They taught me all I knew):—
Their names are What *and* Why *and* When
And How *and* Where *and* Who.

—Rudyard Kipling (1886-1946)

5: The Quest for Clarity

Introduction

How many times have you taken a photograph that might have won a prize if only it had been in focus? Such experiences have probably happened to all of us.

But photographs are not the only things than can be out of focus. Writing can be out of focus, too — and unfortunately often is.

What can we do to ensure that our writing stays in sharp focus?

Well, it's never easy. But this checklist should help:

1. Aim directly, with a specific purpose, at a central subject. (The analogy to picture-taking is clear.)

2. Omit all extraneous material.

3. Emphasize the important attributes of the subject. If necessary, give examples.

4. Play down the less important material. If you keep the really important items in sharp focus, you can permit the lesser ones to get a bit "softer." Just be sure they don't get "fuzzy" instead.

The trick is to take the time to think before you write, just as you might "frame" a picture in your mind before you actually shoot it.

Clarity is everything

In football coach George Allen's game, winning is everything. In our game, clarity is everything. Strive for the crisp, sharp focus we have been talking about. Strive always and unremittingly. Remember, our goal is to avoid any possibility of MISunderstanding. Admittedly, that's an impossible goal. Writing, like law, is far from being an exact science. The best efforts we can manage will still be none too good. But if Robert Browning will forgive me, "A person's reach should exceed a person's grasp, or what's a Heaven for?"

If you keep trying hard to apply the principles learned so far, you will at least be headed in the right direction. Remember, simply cutting excess verbiage will help your readers. But brevity isn't everything. It doesn't help to boil down so much that you omit vital details. Good writing, in the final analysis, is simply clear thinking on paper.

Few writers succeed at this all the time. Some never even come close. But one thing is sure: none of us will ever fight our way down to anywhere near the goal line if we're not in there trying all the time.

Think every problem through. Then explain it in the most logical way you can conjure up. Try using the trick many professional writers rely on: think hard about the subject, then relax and let your subconscious mind take over. You'd be surprised how well this works. And that's why I chose the words "conjure up." They are more apt here than you might have thought.

Once you've put some ideas down on paper, ask yourself a series of questions, based on Kipling's six honest serving men:

- Does this tell *who* is responsible for doing whatever is required?
- Does it explain clearly *what* is supposed to be done?
- Does it tell *when? where? how? why?* And finally,
- Does all this really say what I intended to say?

Those are the questions a good reporter would ask. Make sure you have answered every one of them. Leave nothing to your reader's imagination.

Don't sacrifice clarity in your quest for speed

At various places throughout this handbook, I advise you to proceed "with all possible dispatch" once you start writing. That's extremely good advice, but I must add a warning here: *never* — repeat — *never* sacrifice clarity in your quest for speed. Remember that clarity must always remain your primary goal. Speed will be no help if you run your reader off the road.

To be clear, you must (excuse my blunt language) know what you are talking about. On top of that, you must know exactly what you want to say about your subject. Even then, you must also have mastered the tricks of the writing trade to the point that you can employ each word with understanding of its individual *denotation* (meaning) and *connotation* (emotional overtones). And finally, you will have to learn to string those individual words together with proper regard for the grammar, rhetoric, and usage of American English. (As mentioned earlier, there are still many writers and editors in government and business who care about such things.)

Abstraction — the enemy of clarity

The term *gobbledygook* was coined by the late Maury Maverick. Undoubtedly, you already know what it means, but one definition is "the language of circumlocution, jargon, and pomposity."

Here's one of my favorite examples, courtesy of an entertaining little book entitled *Gobbledygook Has Got to Go*. (Available from the Superintendent of Documents, U.S. Government Printing Office.) It tells about a memo issued early in World War II to instruct federal workers on what to do in case of an air raid. The memo went like this·

"Such preparation shall be made as will completely obscure all Federal buildings and non-Federal buildings occupied by the Federal Government during an air raid for any period of time from visibility by reason of internal or external illumination. Such obscuration may be obtained by blackout construction or by termination of the illumination."

Here's how F.D.R. dignified the memo by giving it simplicity:

"Tell them," President Roosevelt wrote, "that in buildings where they will have to keep the work going to put something over the windows; and, in buildings where they can let the work stop for a while, turn out the lights."

If this kind of unpompous, simple writing means a loss of dignity, then we know a whole lot of readers who wish a lot of writers would lose a lot of "dignity" writing this way. F.D.R. did it all the time. Once, when Frances Perkins was getting a speech ready for him, she wrote this line: "We are endeavoring to construct a more inclusive society."

That night when F.D.R. read the line on the radio, it came out this way: "We are going to make a country in which no one is left out."

Use the right name for things

To write precisely, you must constantly guard against using abstract words that other persons can interpret in different ways. Never use an *abstract* word when you can use a more precise, easily pictured and harder-to-misunderstand *concrete* word.

Words are symbols. The celebrated grammarian Otto Jespersen once said "A word is a human habit." Language relates to the real world much the way a roadmap relates to the territory it depicts. A road map is a system of conventions and symbols. Map readers must know and understand the symbols, or they are just as lost as if they didn't have a map at all.

Words, then, like maps, can have degrees of abstraction. The word *machine*, for example, covers a wide variety of devices — different in purpose, size, shape, and an almost endless list of other things. Nevertheless, the word *machine* undoubtedly brings a picture or a concept to your mind. The picture it evokes for me may be quite different. Still, somehow there are enough common elements that we can communicate, however vaguely.

Mind you, I am not knocking abstraction — we couldn't do without it. Indeed, the ability to abstract probably lies at the root of all human knowledge, and certainly at the root of human language. Without abstractions, we wouldn't be able to communicate. What's more, we probably wouldn't have anything worth communicating.

The ladder of abstraction

Early in life we learn that many English words have several different meanings. A child learns to define those words — and those various meanings — as an individual, through experience. Consequently, if I try to define *my* terms for you, the reader, I can't be sure you'll accept my definitions. You've had experiences of your own; you're quite likely to prefer your own definitions. Frankly, I don't blame you.

Our best hope of reaching a common ground is to use concrete, specific words as often as we can — words that narrow and control the mental images produced. Words having a sensory base are most likely to communicate what we intend. That is to say, words representing objects the reader can see, hear, touch, taste, or smell.

Structural linguists and semanticists have a ball with this subject, and (would you believe I am saying this) their findings make a lot of sense. They have given us a method of coding different meanings of the same word, but that's a bit complex to go into here. They have given us another concept — both simpler and more useful — that I'll pass on to you.

Look at the illustration. The lower rungs of the ladder represent the concrete terms the reader can easily identify in terms of physical senses. Ascending the ladder, you'll find each word becomes more abstract than the one just below it. At the same time, each reference grows more general, more vague, and — accordingly — more open to different interpretations.

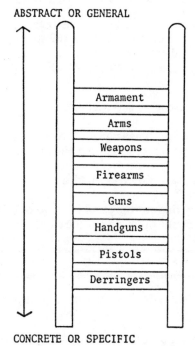

ABSTRACT OR GENERAL

Armament

Arms

Weapons

Firearms

Guns

Handguns

Pistols

Derringers

CONCRETE OR SPECIFIC

ladder of abstraction

As mentioned earlier, abstract words are invaluable. We can't get along without them; I certainly don't want to purge them from your vocabulary. But I would suggest that, in your writing, you link your abstractions to specific experiences by using *examples, analogies,* and *illustrations.* Even better, replace the abstractions with concrete, sensory-style words as often as you can. The more abstract words you use, the harder your copy is to understand. Concrete words make the writing more readable and the meaning more specific.

PRINCIPLE FOUR: Be specific. Use concrete terms in-stead of generalizations.

`Now let's try an easy exercise in levels of abstraction:

Preliminary Exercise: Abstract vs. Concrete Words

In the following sentences, change the abstract words into more concrete or specific terms. Please don't look at the suggestions for rewrites until you have completed your own versions. And remember that, as usual, there aren't any "right" or "wrong" ways to do any of the sentences in this exercise.

1. The housewife purchased several items of food for which she had to pay a high price.
2. The young man read a magazine until very late yesterday evening.
3. The workman placed his tools into a big container.
4. We had a talk about a controversial issue.
5. We went downtown last week, had dinner at a restaurant, and later attended a concert.
6. My pet ran away this morning and a friend of mine found him in an unusual place clear on the other side of the city.

Suggested Rewrites for Preliminary Exercise: Abstract vs. Concrete Words

1. Mrs. Trudy Brown purchased bread, meat, and potatoes, and her bill was $27.80. (Maybe you were even more specific than that: what kind of bread, what kind of meat, what kind of potatoes, etc. And maybe you even put in an additional clue to the reader about the price being high. You might have said something like " . . . and her bill was exorbitant — $27.80." Get the idea?)
2. Teenager Bill Jones read *Newsweek* until 10:00 o'clock yesterday evening. (Maybe you mentioned a specific day.)
3. The plumber placed two monkey wrenches, a blowtorch, and a pipethreader into a large steel toolbox.
4. Albert Kincaid and I had an argument last night about the pros and cons of enforced busing.

5. My cousin Engelbert and I went to downtown Washington last week, had dinner at the Rive Gauche, and later attended a piano recital at the Kennedy Center Concert Hall. (You can tell I made that one up. We really had dinner at McDonald's and heard a free concert by the U.S. Army Band on the Capitol steps.)

6. My pet alligator Hubert ran away and my friend Alfonso found him sunning on a fire escape at the Singles Towers condominium on Beltsville Road.

That ought to do it for now. If you need more practice, you'll find another exercise in Part Three of this handbook, page 195.

Principle Four:

BE SPECIFIC

Use Concrete Terms Instead of Generalizations

Principle Five:

Place modifiers
as close as possible
to the words
they are intended
to modify.

Principle Six:

Avoid unnecessary shifts
of number,
tense,
subject,
voice,
or
point of view.

Of all the faults found in writing,
the wrong placing of words is one of
the most common, and perhaps it leads
to the greatest number of misconceptions.

— William Cobbett (1762-1835)

6: The Quest for Precision

Introduction

Frankly, all I know about William Cobbett is that he was an English writer who used the nom de plume "Peter Porcupine." That has a nice ring to it. Also, whatever else he knew or didn't know about good writing, he was absolutely right about the improper placing of words.

Word order is far more important in the English language than in any other language I know of. Most other European languages are *inflected*; that is to say, a word changes its form according to the part that word is playing in a sentence. The inflection usually involves adding a prefix or a suffix to a "root" word. From these inflections, or special beginnings or endings, the reader can readily tell if a word is the subject of a sentence, a direct object, a possessive, and so on.

From second-year Latin, I recall the first line of Caesar's *Gallic Wars* (just about the only thing I recall from second-year Latin). The line goes: *Gallia est omnis divisa in partes tres.* The translation, for you of today's generation, is "All Gaul is divided into three parts." But I am told that old Julius had a lot of options open to him. He could just as easily have written *Omnis Gallia in tres partes divisa est* and his intended meaning would have remained unchanged. Neat.

As you undoubtedly know, English used to be inflected, too, back in the "olden days." (My kids think I was there.) If you've ever had to study Chaucer's *Canterbury Tales,* you have discovered that you had to expend almost the same effort as if you were learning a new and foreign language. Yet Chaucer's language is much more closely akin to our present English than was the "Old English" or "Anglo-Saxon" of yet earlier times. If you've read any of *Beowulf,* you remember that the language of that epic poem was really more closely related to some of the Germanic languages than it is to our modern English.

But the English language has from its beginnings always been growing and changing. Some of the more extreme changes came after the Norman invasion of 1066. Since then, the language of the British Isles received an infusion of Romance-root words to take their places beside Anglo-Saxon words. What we now call Modern English became gloriously enriched in the process. We now have at least two words, and usually more, for just about everything. But, as the language grew in vocabulary, it also began to change in other ways at an increasingly rapid rate.

The importance of word order in the English language

By Shakespeare's time, many inflections had begun to disappear. And how much more the language has changed since then. Today, when modern readers attempt *Hamlet,* or *Romeo and Juliet,* they must make a special study of the archaic language of The Bard before they can understand it fully.

Yes, the grammatical construction of English today is in many ways much simpler than it used to be. But we have paid a price for losing the language's inflections; now we must pay more and more attention to arranging words in their proper order. If today's writers deviate from the so-called "natural" word order of subject-verb-object (our friendly structural linguists say S-V-O), or subject-verb-complement, they run a strong risk of being misunderstood.

In my youth I was a dedicated fan of the "Gashouse Gang" — the St. Louis Cardinals of the late 1930s. So I am still faintly embarrassed at quoting one of their old archrivals from the Brooklyn Bums — Eddie Stanky, "the Brat." But Stanky had a saying he often used that demonstrates what I'm talking about, so here goes: *"It ain't the size of the dog in the fight, it's the size of the fight in the dog."*

Note that essentially the same words are used in both halves of the sentence — but they mean very different things. Word order is the key.

For good measure, here's another example: *The dogcatcher chased the dog. The dog chased the dogcatcher.*

Same words in each sentence. Totally different meaning.

Ambiguity

Murphy's Law is true in spades when it comes to interpreting ambiguous statements. If a sentence can possibly be misunderstood, it will be. And improper word order is probably the greatest cause of double (and triple) meanings. An adjective will do its utmost to attach itself to the nearest noun; an adverb will do the same to the nearest verb, adjective, adverb, or sometimes even the nearest clause.

Remember — if you put any modifier near a word or phrase that might be considered "eligible" for modification, but isn't the real one to be modified, you will inevitably mislead the reader.

PRINCIPLE FIVE: Keep related sentence elements together; keep unrelated elements apart. Place modifiers as close as possible to the words they are intended to modify.

Observe that the problem often does not lie with the modifiers themselves; they may be perfectly all right. It's the company they keep.

Misplaced modifiers

Watch out especially for *misplaced modifiers* — that is to say, modifying words or phrases that appear to modify one word in a sentence, but actually are intended to modify another. Consider the difference, for example, between "We *almost* lost our entire investment," and "We lost *almost* our entire investment." Version one means that the entire investment was almost lost, but was not. Version two means that the greater part of the entire investment was indeed lost.

Here's one with a misplaced phrase instead of a single word. Compare "He polished the beautiful Mercedes-Benz his father had given to him *with tender care,*" and "He polished *with tender care* the beautiful Mercedes-Benz his father had given to him." See the difference?

Look out for "only"

The word "only" is one of the trickiest in the English language. Some years ago I ran across an interesting sentence. By changing the position of the single word *only* you could change the shade of meaning of the entire sentence. Sometimes the meaning changed a little — other times quite drastically. I no longer remember the source of this exercise, sorry to say, but — with appropriate thanks to the person who devised it — here is the way it goes:

1. *Only* John mourned the death of his brother. (This means that no one else — only John — mourned . . .)
2. John *only* mourned the death of his brother. (This is what English teachers call a "squinting" construction. The *only* could modify either *John* or *mourned*. We often use this kind of word order in speech, and are seldom misunderstood. In writing, however, we must be more careful; strive for a more precise placement. It isn't really all that much trouble.)
3. John mourned *only* the death of his brother. (This means that John had the deep feeling of mourning only for his brother; he may have felt slightly sad about the death of others.)
4. John mourned the death of his *only* brother. (Means that he had but one brother.)
5. John mourned the death of his brother *only*. (Means much the same as sentence 3, but with increased emphasis on the *only*, since it is the final word in the sentence.)

In fairness, I must tell you that I may be nitpicking on this. Some of the most respected American authorities on usage are not nearly this fussy about the placement of the word "only." They believe that in colloquial English it is perfectly all right to say, for example, "He only spent a dollar," rather than "He spent only a dollar." I respectfully disagree — at least in the context of the intent of this book. If we are truly concerned with accuracy, and with avoiding ambiguity, we had better watch where we put this slippery word.

Another constantly misused phrase is "not all." You've seen a jillion television commercials in which the statement is made that "All toothpastes (or mouthwashes, or dog foods, or whatever) are not alike." Wrong! The correct structure for that kind of sentence is "Not all toothpastes are alike."

Dangling modifiers

There are several different kinds of dangling constructions, but the faults are similar in all of them. For those of you who remember your formal English grammar, they can be dangling *gerund* phrases, *participial* phrases, or *infinitive* phrases. Actually, you can get along quite well in life without knowing these things. A *gerund* and a *participle* look exactly alike; both have "-ing" endings. The first is used as a *noun,* the second as an *adjective,* just in case you've forgotten the distinction. You very likely do remember that an *infinitive* is a form of the verb preceded by the *sign of the infinitive,* the preposition *to. (To go, to talk, to walk,* etc.)

Phrases are said to dangle when they do not clearly and logically refer to the appropriate noun or pronoun.

Here is a dangling gerund phrase: *After climbing the mountain, the view was beautiful.* The view didn't climb the mountain. Change this to something like *After climbing the mountain, we saw a beautiful view.* In other words, add a noun or pronoun for the dangling phrase to modify. Or, if you desire, you can change the phrase to a clause or an *absolute* construction. Say something like *After we climbed the mountain, we saw a beautiful view.* (The trick is to give the clause its own subject.)

Here's a dangling participial phrase: *Moving to Arizona, his rheumatism quickly improved.* (The rheumatism didn't move to Arizona — or at least, not as a separate entity.) Change this one to read: *After moving to Arizona, he found that his rheumatism quickly improved.* Or: *After his move [or moving] to Arizona, his rheumatism quickly improved.*

Here's a dangling infinitive phrase: *To save money, the thermostat must be turned down to 68 degrees.* Change that to something like *To save money, you must turn the thermostat down to 68 degrees.*

Squinting modifiers

A modifier is said to "squint" when it can be interpreted as modifying either of two (or more) sentence elements. The reader will be confused, or perhaps totally unable to decipher which meaning the writer intends. Usually it's a matter of not being able to tell whether to look forward (that is, toward the end of the sentence) or backward (toward the beginning). Look at this example:

Dr. Jones instructed his patient while in the hospital to watch his diet very carefully. Think about this one. Did the doctor do the instructing while his patient was hospitalized? Or did the doctor instruct his patient to watch his diet during the period that he was going to be in the hospital? Either interpretation is possible.

You could rewrite this by saying something such as *Dr. Jones instructed his patient to watch his diet very carefully during the time he was in the hospital.* Or, another interpretation: *While visiting his patient in the hospital, Dr. Jones instructed him to watch his diet very carefully.*

Exercises:

You will find exercises on Misplaced Modifiers and Dangling Modifiers in Section Three, page 196.

Consistency

Clarity and precision in writing require consistency. Your reader will have a much easier time comprehending quickly what you have written if you are consistent in your approach. (Keeping this in mind will also help you to organize your points.) Try to stick to one point of view, one subject, until there is a definite need to change it. When a change is needed, start a new paragraph.

PRINCIPLE SIX: Avoid unnecessary shifts of number, tense, subject, voice, or point of view.

Many different kinds of shifts are lumped under this one heading, for — although they are all different — in many ways they are all very much alike. The basic principle is simple: don't throw your reader any curves. If you start out down a particular path, don't constantly twist and turn. Keep going right straight ahead, and if you *must* turn, at least give the reader as much warning as you can.

Watch out particularly for:

a. Shift of number.

Careless writers have always been inclined to write such things as "Everyone should save *their* money." As you can see, the subject, *everyone,* is a singular noun. Harking back to the rules of grammar you learned in grade school days, you know that a pronoun is supposed to agree with its antecedent in number. The word *their* is obviously plural, and hence does not agree with the singular subject. Why, then, do so many writers constantly employ this kind of construction?

Probably we can ascribe this in part, at least, to the advent of the women's movement. Writers don't want to appear sexist, so they use the plural form *their,* which has no connotation of sex, even though they are aware that the construction is incorrect. They don't want to have to say *his,* which would be grammatically correct, but sexist. They feel that *his/her* looks and sounds awkward. (I agree.) So they choose what they consider to be the lesser of the evils, and write the plural form *their.* Thus, they avoid sexism, but in the process they break the rules of grammar. Granted, it's a dilemma.

Most of the time, though there's an easy way out. All you have to do is use a *plural* form of the word up front, as the subject. Then you can legitimately use *their* as the pronoun. Thus, instead of writing "Everyone should save *his* money," or worse, "Everyone should save *his/her* money," why not try something like "People should save *their* money." See how painless it is? And you've violated no rules of English grammar.

Of course, this device doesn't always work — after all, nothing's perfect. But, in the few cases when it won't work, there are other ways. We won't go into them here, but for some other possible solutions, refer to the *he/she dilemma* in the handbook section.

b. Shift of tense. This mistake, while also a very common one, usually stems more from carelessness than from ignorance. A writer will be going merrily along, and suddenly and inconsistently change tenses, for no good reason. "When he heard about the accident he screams and cries like a baby." This kind of error is very easy to correct. Simply put all verbs in the same tense: "When he heard about the accident he screamed and cried like a baby."

c. Shift of subject. "Abraham Lincoln was born in Kentucky, but Illinois was his home in later years." To correct this, make the subject of one verb the subject of both verbs: "Abraham Lincoln was born in Kentucky, but lived in Illinois in later years." (Or, if you really want to have the states as subjects, you could say something like this: "Kentucky was the birthplace of Abraham Lincoln, but Illinois was his home in later years.")

A few explanations and cautions are probably in order here. Do not let this "rule" hogtie or inhibit you. Actually, it is really very flexible, and is often broken by even the best and most careful writers. Mostly the problems come when the subject is changed within a compound sentence. It's okay to change the subject in a complex sentence, and often it would be difficult not to. Don't worry about it.

One other thing. Don't let this rule inhibit you when you change, for example, the direct object of one sentence to the subject of the next. This construction has a long and honorable history. Remember one of the first Mother Goose rhymes you learned as a child. "The farmer takes a wife. The wife takes the child. The child takes the dog. The dog takes the cat. The cat takes the rat." And so on. There is nothing wrong with this, and indeed, it is frequently a useful way of keeping the reader on the track.

d. Shift of voice. This, too, is a common error. It's no great crime, but it doesn't contribute to clarity and reader understanding. Let's consider a typical example: "If a coach wishes to win the respect of his team, a firm discipline must be maintained." (Notice that the sentence begins in the active voice, then shifts to the passive halfway through.) Simply put both verbs in the active voice: "If a coach wishes to win the respect of his team, he must maintain a firm discipline." (Of course, both the original sentence and the rewrite are sexist, so let's try one more time: "If coaches wish to win the respect of their teams, they must maintain a firm discipline.")

e. Shift in point of view. "When you look through the microscope, the cell divides to form two organisms." Even the logic is faulty in this one, since the cell is going to divide whether you are watching it or not. To correct the sentence (and the logic) give both clauses the same subject: "When you look through the microscope, you can see the cell divide to form two organisms."

Exercise:

You will find an exercise on Unnecessary Shifts in Section Three, page 197.

The difference between the right word and the almost right word is the difference between lightning and a lightning bug.

—Mark Twain (1835-1910)

7: The Right Word

Introduction

The right word is usually the simple word. H.W. Fowler, one of my heroes, put it like this: "Prefer the familiar word to the far fetched. . . Prefer the short word to the long. Prefer the Saxon word to the Romance." (*The King's English,* p. 11.)

Fowler went on to explain that the principles he listed were "roughly in order of merit," and that "the last is also the least." By all means read his full explanation; you'll enjoy it. Suffice it to say here that Fowler wasn't exhibiting a prejudice against Latin-based words. As he himself pointed out, the Romance word may well be the "right word" in many instances. Indeed, the French language has exactly the right words for "exactly the right word" — the word writers and editors are supposed to be constantly looking for, but can't always find. The French call it "le mot juste."

Fowler's main point is that Saxon-root words are usually shorter. Latin-root words, often incorporating prefixes and suffixes, are much more likely to be polysyllabic. (Several words in the previous sentence demonstrate the point admirably.)

Choosing the "right word"

How does a writer choose the right word? Sometimes the process is arduous. Obviously, a person with a good vocabulary has a much better chance of finding an appropriate word than does another person having fewer words to choose from.

If, as many psychologists believe, vocabulary is one indicator of intelligence, making a conscious effort to improve one's vocabulary is probably not a bad idea. *Reader's Digest* has had a monthly feature on this subject for many years. And while it's long been a popular sport among the literary intelligentsia to put down the *Digest,* I'll unhesitatingly take the other side. If you want to find examples of clear, tightly edited prose, you'll look a long way to hunt down anything better than you can encounter in any issue of the much maligned *Reader's Digest.*

Good English is appropriate English

As everyone knows, people talk and write at different "levels" according to the situation. If you're talking with friends at a party or a picnic, for example, you'll use one level. If you make a formal presentation to the Board of Directors, you'll use another. And there are other levels in between.

Is one level "better English" than another? Linguistic scholars don't believe so, and they are probably right. English is not "good" if it is out of place; using Board-of-Directors language at the corner bar might get someone a horselaugh, or maybe even a punch in the nose.

The point is that good English, so-called, is *language that is appropriate to the situation.* The language spoken at Joe's Bar is what the late H.L. Mencken called "vulgate" English (from the Latin word for *popular* or common). Mencken chose that term because none of the other descriptive words in use at the time filled the bill. Some scholars were calling such English "vulgar," but to many persons that word carries a connotation different from the one intended. The term "illiterate," once in vogue, wasn't much better — it implies "unable to read or write." And the terms "popular" or "folk" make such English appear more acceptable than it usually is when it is employed in the world of business, industry, or government.

One notch above "vulgate" comes informal English. (Structural linguists might say one type of language is not "above" another. Nevertheless, the word "level" implies "higher" and "lower" to most people, probably including the scholars themselves.) Informal English, the level most people use in conversation, can be carried over to some extent in our everyday writing. Obviously, some levels overlap considerably, particularly in the subgroups of language called *slang, jargon,* and *shoptalk.* The last two terms describe the vocabulary — often consisting of a sort of verbal shorthand — used by persons in the same occupation.

At the top of the ladder comes "formal" English. More often written than spoken, it is used primarily by highly educated persons addressing their peers. Some element of snobbery is probably involved, but let's not make any educational or social judgments. Suffice it to say that *formal writing* has its place. But *business writing* — intended to communicate with, and be understood by, the general public — is *not* that place. For those concerned more with communication than with elegance, formal writing may seem overly confining. That's bad enough, but to readers it is even more restrictive; it interferes with their natural right to comprehend.

Business writing should consist of good *informal* English. That is, it should be much like informal speech, but with tighter sentence structure and more precise expression.

PRINCIPLE SEVEN: Prefer the simple word to the far-fetched, and the right word to the almost right.

Principle Seven:

Prefer the simple word to the far-fetched,

and the right word to the almost right.

The evils of elegant variation

"Elegant variation" is a term coined by H.W. Fowler to describe a device writers sometimes use to avoid repeating a word — usually they set an arbitrary limit, such as within the same sentence, within 20 words, or within a paragraph. They do this because, somewhere along the way, they've been brainwashed into believing that there is a "rule" *never* to use the same word twice in the same sentence.

Used sensibly, the "rule" isn't a bad one. Unfortunately, many writers don't use it sensibly. Listen to a broadcast of sports scores any evening, and you'll probably hear at some time one of the following elegant variations: *The Redskins emerged victorious; the Colts romped to victory; the Cowboys slaughtered the opposition; the Dolphins clobbered their opponents;* and so on, ad nauseam. Up to a certain point it can be amusing. That point is quickly reached; after that, the entire technique becomes at best boring — at worst, ridiculous.

Leave it to elegant writers to use elegant variations. In *useful* writing, such variations often mislead the reader. Suppose, for example, that the same individual is both the president and the treasurer of an organization. A writer striving for elegant variation might write something like this: *The president announced that the company had completed a very successful year. Treasurer Jones said there had been a profit of $3.25 a share.*

The reader would be led to believe that the president and the treasurer are two separate persons. Thus, it would be far better to refer to the individual by the same title (or *both* titles, if you prefer), even at the risk of repetition. And with a little care, even that can be avoided. How about this: *Mr. Jones, president and treasurer, announced that the company had completed a very successful year, with a profit of $3.25 a share.*

In useful writing, don't let yourself be handcuffed by this so-called rule against elegant variation. You're the boss. Here's the principle you should follow:

PRINCIPLE EIGHT: Don't repeat a word or words un – necessarily. But don't hesitate to repeat when the repetition will increase clarity.

Exercises:
Exercises involving problems of Unnecessary Repetition and Elegant Variation can be found in Part Three, page 199.

Reference Works

Dictionaries

If you can't find "le mot juste" in your working vocabulary, what's the next step? Some writers will turn immediately to such references as *Roget's Thesaurus, Webster's Dictionary of Synonyms,* or *Rodale's Word Finder.* We'll discuss such works later. Right now, let's begin with the book most writers reach for first — the dictionary.

A generation ago, *"the* dictionary" meant just one thing: the *Merriam-Webster New Second International Dictionary,* or its desk-sized junior partner, *Webster's Collegiate.* True, there were other dictionaries — good ones — but the *Second* was considered by most American writers and scholars to be the final authority on American English.

Unfortunately, few of today's writers are willing to say the same thing about its present-day successor, the *Third International.* Even though the *Third* is a work of towering linguistic scholarship, it would appear to be written more for linguistic scholars than for the rest of us —that is to say, the vast majority of the human race.

The *Third* is by design a *descriptive* rather than a *prescriptive* work. Its makers explain that they are concerned with *describing the way people use words;* they say it is not in their province to *prescribe* how people are *supposed* to use words.

There are many good reasons for such an approach; the linguists advance some very persuasive arguments. And certainly they have a right to do things that way if they want to. My complaint is that most of us who are not linguistic scholars go to the dictionary because we seek authoritative answers to our questions. *Most of us, I feel sure, really want a PRESCRIPTION, not a DESCRIPTION.* At least we want some guidelines, some indications of how persons deeply concerned with language would use a particular word or phrase.

Is there evidence for this, or is it simply my opinion? Well, you might be surprised to know how many working writers are still using battered but cherished copies of the *Second International,* even though it hasn't been updated since the 1930s. The *Second* does not, of course, define any of the thousands of new words that have entered the language since its publication: for example, the whole vocabularies of the nuclear energy and space programs. But working writers still like the way the *Second* is put together; that's why even a dog-eared copy costs more secondhand than the *Third* costs brand new.

My old mentor (I have chosen both those words with great precision), Mazie Worcester, has promised me her copy of the *Second* if she shuffles off this mortal coil before I do. I mention that here, in print, because I know she has many other friends who covet that book and plan to do me out of it if they can. Let the record show she has promised it to me!

Okay, back to business. Since it's unlikely most of you can locate a copy of the *Second,* or would be willing to lay out that much money if you do happen to find one, what's your alternative?

Well, you have several. Let's mention a few of the new dictionaries that are very good indeed. In my opinion, your best buy is probably the paperback edition of *The American Heritage Dictionary*. If you use it as much as I do, however, you'll quickly wear it out. So you might want to spend a bit more and get the hardback edition. (No, they aren't paying me a commission.)

Another good candidate is *The Random House Dictionary of the English Language*. Many writers swear by it. Both *Random House* and *American Heritage* are described as "unabridged," but actually are not. They would have to contain many more words — or, in dictionary talk, "entries," — to qualify for that description.

As a matter of fact, the *Third International* can't truly claim to be unabridged either. It omits all proper names (there is a separate dictionary for those); but what's far worse, its editors have eliminated thousands of words because they have decreed them to be "archaic." The catch is that much of the language of Shakespeare and the King James Bible falls into that category. Archaic? Ridiculous! Educated persons will need to know those "archaic" words for as long as the English language exists. Excluding such words is shortsighted, to say the least.

So if you really feel the need for an unabridged dictionary, get the *Oxford English Dictionary*. There's no risk in saying the *Oxford* is far and away the greatest English language dictionary in the world. The full-sized edition comes in multiple volumes and is a masterpiece of scholarship and completeness. But even it has its drawbacks: it is bulky, very expensive, and very "British." You can get around the first two drawbacks by buying the "MICRO" version; it contains the same information, but reduced in type size to fit into two volumes. The print is minuscule in the true sense of that word, but the publishers thoughtfully have furnished a powerful reading glass to go with it. (No, they don't pay me a commission either.)

One other comment about dictionaries before we move on.

If you love language, you probably also love dictionaries. You're in the habit of looking words up, and that's good. It helps ensure knowing not only what you *think* a word means, but also — far more important — what the word is likely to mean to others. What we need is to get an insight into the difference between *denotation* — the way a word is defined — and *connotation* — the emotional overtones that often accompany the word. Many words that appear acceptable to readers if interpreted according to strict definition might actually be considered discourteous or offensive to many because of the underlying connotation. Writers, beware.

We must always be aware of dictionary meanings, of course. Look words up if you have any doubt about them. But learn to look past the formal definition. Using a word with bad connotations can evoke strong emotion you'd sooner leave unstirred. For shades of meaning and *connotation,* you'll find some other books are even more useful than a regular dictionary.

References on Usage, Shades of Meaning, and Connotations of Words

One of the most helpful references on this subject was published in 1976. It is the *Harper Dictionary of Contemporary Usage,* edited by William and Mary Morris.

What makes this book different — and valuable — is that the Morrises are concerned with the English used by writers, editors, teachers, and others who care about precision. They accordingly chose a panel of more than 130 experts — novelists, poets, scholars, and even a Supreme Court Justice noted for writing more clearly than most of his distinguished but verbose colleagues.

To find out what these experts think about word usages, the Morrises began sending them questionnaires, starting back in 1971. They carefully chose words about which opinions often differed strongly; then they asked the experts to comment. The panelists voted as to whether they would use a particular word in speech or in writing; often they commented as well.

The book makes fascinating reading. Some of the comments are pungent, some enlightening, and some funny. For example:

Is there a distinction between "flaunt" and "flout" — used interchangeably by two court justices — worth preserving?

Michael J. Arlen, writer: "I should damn well hope so." Ben Lucien Burman, novelist: "No wonder Roosevelt wanted to fire the Supreme Court!" Stanley Kunitz, poet: "I flout those who flaunt their ignorance." [Comment: Beautiful!]

May "author" be a verb?

Saul Bellow, author: "No, nor the word 'crafted.' Abominable!" Herman Wouk, novelist: "No, no, no, no, no, no, no, no! NO!"

Berton Rouché, writer, voting no: "Why should error be approved? [My comment: Amen.]

How about 'giving input' to the President?

Lewis Mumford, author: "Input has a legitimate use in computerdom. Otherwise it should be shunned. It is the equivalent of y'know for those who don't know the right word." Berton Rouché, author: "I accept 'output', but — I don't know why — input turns my stomach. Maybe it's the people who use such words." Pierre Berton, author: "I do not mingle socially with people who talk that way and would not expect my readers to stick with me if I used it." Peter DeVries: " . . .the thought of putting information into a President is a little grotesque." Red Smith: "This usage brings a violent output of nausea here. Couldn't the President have access to advice instead?"

Well, that's enough to give you the flavor of the book.

If there is one reference work other than the dictionary that word-conscious writers refer to constantly, it is probably *Roget's Thesaurus.* This useful work is available in many sizes and shapes. The version I use most of the time is called *The New Roget's Thesaurus in Dictionary Form,* edited by Norman Lewis. If you don't have some kind of thesaurus, you should remedy that situation right away.

Another good word reference is *Webster's Dictionary of Synonyms.* I suspect it has even more words than *Roget's.*

A slightly different approach can be found in a series of works published some years ago by the late J. I. Rodale. A self-educated man and noted health food enthusiast, Rodale was fascinated with words: he commissioned a group of scholars to help him put together *The Word-Finder, The Adjective-Finder,* and *The Adverb-Finder.* Some or all of these are probably out of print now, but perhaps might be found secondhand. They are worth looking for. One of the good things about *The Word-Finder* is that it suggests combinations of words — adverbs and adjectives to go with particular nouns, for example.

The reference I await most eagerly is to be called *The Dictionary's Companion.* This is the as yet unpublished brainchild of my friend and colleague, Virgil Carrington "Pat" Jones. Pat has been working on this ambitious project for years, with rigorous attention to every detail. He has come up with the most elaborate word reference (and cross-reference) book I have ever seen. Even the synonyms for a given word are themselves listed alphabetically. When Pat says it is a "completely alphabetized word finder," he isn't kidding. It is, as the bookjacket copy will say, "The book Noah Webster did not have time to write . . . as necessary as a period at the end of a sentence." When it comes off the press, I hope to be standing at the head of the line to buy the first copy. I wish I had it now.

Since I don't have it (and you can't get it yet either), let me tell you about another very helpful reference that I've just discovered. Suppose you know the definition of a word you want, but can't think of the word itself — has this happened to you? Welcome to the group. Well, Theodore Bernstein has come up with the answer to our problem: a new dictionary called *The Reverse Dictionary*. I've had my copy only a short time, but have already found it extremely helpful. It really gives you a handle on all those words you know you know, but can't think of when you need them. Mr. Bernstein, congratulations on a great idea!

Principle Eight:

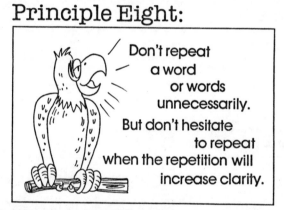

Don't repeat
a word
or words
unnecessarily.
But don't hesitate
to repeat
when the repetition will
increase clarity.

Other Valuable Reference Works

A Dictionary of Contemporary American Usage, by Bergen and Cornelia Evans.

Writer's Guide and Index to English, by Porter Perrin.

Modern American Usage, by Wilson Follett, edited and completed by Jacques Barzun.

Modern English Usage, by H. W. Fowler (or the American English version by Margaret Nicholson).

The Merriam-Webster Pocket Dictionary of Proper Names, compiled by Geoffrey Payton.

EXERCISE:

An exercise on preferring the Simple Word can be found in Part Three, page 198.

Principle Nine:

Make sentence elements
that are parallel
in thought
parallel in form.
But
do not use parallelism
to express thoughts
that are not parallel.

Principle Ten:

Arrange your material logically
Always begin with ideas
the reader can readily
understand.

If you must present
difficult material
go one step at a time.
Arrange your format
to give the reader every
possible "handle"
on the material.

In whatever paragraphs or essays you write, verify the sequence of ideas and take out or transpose everything that interrupts the march of thought and feeling.

— *Jacques Barzun,* Simple and Direct

8: How to Make Order out of Chaos

Introduction

There are many stylistic and grammatical devices available to improve and clarify the communication process — the process of transferring thoughts from the mind of the writer to the mind of the reader. Among the most useful of these devices is the one teachers of English call "parallelism," or "parallel construction."

Parallelism

Parallelism is neither complicated nor difficult. All you need to know is that you can show the similarity of certain thoughts or ideas by using similar grammatical constructions in a number of successive units — whether those units be words, phrases, clauses, sentences, paragraphs, or even longer units.

Let's illustrate the virtues of parallelism by listing them in a parallel construction, thus:

Parallelism is a useful device that can:
● *tidy up thoughts or ideas;*
● *clarify relationships;*

● *straighten out mixed-up phrases, clauses, or sentences;*

● *convert entire paragraphs, pages, sections, or chapters from chaos to order; and*

● *unify entire documents or books.*

Parallelism has a strong appeal to the reader's sense of order. To a person educated in the proper usage of language, hardly anything sounds quite so disorganized in writing as structure that is not made parallel when it should be. Compare these two sentences:

NOT PARALLEL: *Briefly, the functions of the executive staff are to advise the president, transmit his instructions, and the supervision of the execution of his decisions.*

PARALLEL: *Briefly, the functions of the executive staff are to advise the president, transmit his instructions, and supervise the execution of his decisions.*

As you can see, parallelism makes for an economical use of words at the same time it is helping to clarify meaning and relationships. In the process it also produces an aesthetic symmetry that pleases the reader's eye. That effect is pure *lagniappe,* a French expression that means something thrown in as a bonus. The slang term in English would be "freebie." It is better not to use foreign words like this, but if you do, explain them, just as I have done here.

Many inexperienced writers think of parallelism only in terms of sentences and paragraphs. That's fine, but why stop there? It's wasteful to ignore the potential benefits that can emerge when the reader can look at the big picture. Parallelism can be enormously useful in putting together an outline, a table of contents, or even a system of headings and subheadings for a long piece of writing. Again, the system helps the reader figure out relative values of items, and how everything fits together.

PRINCIPLE NINE. Make sentence elements that are parallel in thought parallel in form. But do not use parallelism to express thoughts that are not parallel.

To express parallel thoughts, match words with words, phrases with phrases, clauses with clauses, or topics with topics. Do NOT match an element with a larger or structurally different element.

NOT PARALLEL: *She began walking back and forth and to frown worriedly.* (Notice the shift from the participle "walking" to the infinitive "to frown.")

PARALLEL: *She began to walk back and forth and (to) frown worriedly.* (Change both to infinitives.) OR *She began walking back and forth and frowning worriedly.* (Both participles.)

Here is another type of nonparallel construction that seems to be particularly common in administrative writing:

The duties of the Secretary of the Women's Association are:
(a) to take minutes of all the meetings; (phrase)
(b) the secretary answers all the correspondence; and (clause)
(c) writing of monthly reports. (topic)

Change this by using all phrases, thus:

The duties of the Secretary of the Women's Association are:
(a) to take minutes of all the meetings;
(b) to answer all the correspondence; and
(c) to write the monthly reports.

OR change it by using all clauses, thus:

Here is a list of the secretary's duties:
(a) she takes minutes of all the meetings;
(b) she answers all the correspondence; and
(c) she writes the monthly reports.

Notice that in addition to the obvious changes involved in using all phrases or all clauses, there is a less obvious one of inserting a "the" in item (c). To make your parallelism clearer and more effective, you'll find it helpful to repeat articles, such as was done in this case, or prepositions, or pronouns, or helping verbs, or signs of the infinitive.

Parallelism is a handy tool for organizing, but it can't do everything. Some other principles — mostly related — are useful in organizing material for maximum reader interest and understanding.

The trick is to take advantage of the human mind's natural capacity for order. How? Simple — if one thing is similar to another, point out the similarity. If it is different, emphasize the difference. And if the two items are related, point out the relationship.

Making logical arrangements

Remember that *no writer can ever tell the whole story about anything.* James Joyce's famous work *Ulysses* takes 783 pages to describe the events of a single day in the lives of a limited number of characters. Even then, masterly as the work is, it gives only a hint of Joyce's admittedly impossible intent. A detailed account of a single hour in the life of a single character could take a conscientious novelist six months or a year to write — perhaps even longer. And the sad part is, it still wouldn't begin to do the job.

So the writer must decide early on what to put in, and — more important — what to leave out. This is a difficult decision. What can be omitted without harming the reader's understanding?

The guidelines are: (a) stick to the essential facts, and *only* those facts; and (b) excise all extraneous material.

Strive constantly to put everything in logical order. Start with basics all readers will understand. Then progress one step at a time until perhaps the reader can arrive eventually at more difficult concepts that were beyond comprehension at the beginning.

> **PRINCIPLE TEN: Arrange your material logically. Always begin with ideas the reader can readily understand. If you must present difficult material, go one step at a time. Do not skip any steps. Arrange your format to give the reader every possible "handle" on the material.**

Let's delve a bit deeper into what makes one arrangement of presentation easier to follow than another. For simplicity, let's consider a one-page document. Later we'll work up to larger projects.

To begin with, let's use one of the abilities that seems to make the human mind unique — the ability to *categorize.* Many psychologists have written that the ability to sort things out is one of the most important tools we have in learning and remembering. Indeed, much of our human knowledge appears to be derived from these skills.

For those of my readers who are as unorganized as I am, this illustration may sound familiar. My wife often asks me to stop by the grocery on my way home from work. She has her own way of making out a grocery list, putting items down as they come to her mind — maybe a quart of milk, a loaf of bread, a head of lettuce, a can of tomatoes, some paper towels, and various other items in no particular order.

Anyone with what Jim Aswell would call "bat sense" would rearrange the list, putting similar things together. Then it would be easy to pick up every item located in a particular department, move on to the next, and so on. Simple logic.

Well, I never remember to do that; once in the grocery I take many an extra step, wandering back and forth from one department to another. I rationalize that all the extra walking gives me some much needed exercise. But in writing, that's exercise you don't need!

The general-to-specific method of development

Probably the best single way of arranging most material for easy understanding is what we call the general-to-specific order. This means that you start with a general statement; then follow up with additional facts that elaborate or explain the statement. This makes it extremely easy for your readers to follow all the way.

For example, the opening statement, "We need to buy a new typewriter," might be supported by the following facts: (a) Our old machine no longer does acceptable work; (b) it is impossible to get replacement parts; and (c) a new machine will quickly pay for itself in time saved and increased quality of work.

The chronological method of development

This method of development, also extremely useful, is a simple one: all you have to do is to discuss events in the same time sequence that they actually occur; start with the first event and proceed chronologically, one event at a time, until the last. The chronological method is almost always the best way to write a history or a biography. It is also frequently used for news stories. And it is almost essential for explaining a process in which time relationships play an important role.

Sometimes, however, the chronological approach is inappropriate. In such cases, it may confuse both writer and reader. We become so used to thinking about almost everything in terms of chronology that we can be trapped into using that approach even when it may keep us from expressing our thoughts clearly.

Suppose, for example, that you're writing a test report on a new aircraft. For heaven's sake, don't start with what happened when the Wright Brothers were at Kitty Hawk. (And don't think I'm exaggerating — some report writers I know would probably start there!) Don't even begin with what happened last year or last month. Remember the important thing is to get straight to the point.

Other methods of arrangement

In a college English Composition course, you would learn many other systems of arrangement. What I have described as "general to specific" would probably be called "deductive order." Its opposite number, "specific to general" is known as "inductive order." You'd also hear about analytical order, spatial order, and perhaps cause-and-effect order. All of these are good to know, but for practical purposes we're going to skip them here. Chances are, you'll never even miss them in your everyday writing projects.

Whatever method you decide is appropriate for a particular project, the following points will be important:

1. *Start with something the reader is familiar with, and interested in.* Then move on, one step at a time. Don't skip any steps. Lead the reader at a comfortable rate from the known to the unknown, or from the general to the specific.

2. *Use analogies, comparisons, contrasts, examples, or illustrations* to help explain any difficult ideas or concepts.

3. *Use the same system all the way through.* That means if you're using measurements, for example, you'll stick to the same kind. Don't use "feet" or "miles" in one section and "meters" or "kilometers" in another. If for some reason you need to use both systems, ordinarily you should give the familiar one first, then use parentheses to convert the figures into the other system. Don't make your reader do the math!

NOTE: If you are working for an organization that's trying to do missionary work by converting readers to the metric system, go ahead and put the metric numbers first; then follow with the conventional U.S. system in parentheses. Ordinarily, this wouldn't be a good arrangement, but circumstances alter cases.

4. *Choose a logic that will be quickly clear to the reader.* For example, if you are discussing four animals — a cat, a dog, a horse, and an elephant — what would be a logical arrangement? Well, according to my logic, at least, the order I just used would be the best one, although you might argue for other ways. *My* logic here is that people usually think in terms of going *from the small to the large,* and might be confused if you started at the other end of the size scale. (The converse would be true if you were discussing items in the microscopic or submicroscopic range.) Also, the first animals listed would be more familiar to most readers.

Another way might be to organize *the individual items into related groups: cats, lions, tigers; coyotes, dogs, and wolves; burros, horses, and mules;* and so on. Observe that the alphabet still works fine in the subsystems, but again, there are other ways.

5. *Work out a suitable layout and format to help the reader.* If you are discussing just three or four items, a narrative paragraph will probably work fine. But if you are dealing with a longer list, you might want to consider tabular form, or numbered or lettered items, so that the dif-

ferences and similarities can readily be contrasted and compared by the reader.

6. *Use tables, graphs, and pictures whenever they seem appropriate.* Many readers will find material much easier to understand in pictorial form. Don't hesitate to augment narrative descriptions with tables, charts, graphs, or other illustrations. Some critics might consider this approach wasteful of space and paper; don't believe them. Some readers are word minded; others are oriented more toward mathematics, engineering, and visual displays. Help both groups, not just one.

7. *Make important items stand out.* Use freely all the typographical devices that are available to you. Employ logic and imagination — the basic aim is to put in *any* kind of device that might help the reader locate important information and relate it to other items for comparison and contrast. That means you can use, at a minimum, all the devices available on a typewriter keyboard: underscore, capital letters, asterisks, filled-in "o's" for bullets, and so forth. If your typewriter has changeable fonts or pitches, you can use these features to great advantage. If your material is to be typeset and printed, that opens a whole new world — different type faces and sizes, different makeups and layouts, and so on.

Whatever the system, you should plan to make maximum use of major and minor headings and subheadings. Also use plenty of "white space," which can help the reader as much or more than many other devices.

Exercise:

An exercise in Orderly Arrangement can be found in Part Three, page 201.

Axiom One:

DO NOT WRITE
WITHOUT
GOOD
REASON.

There are only two tests for telling whether a letter is too long. One is whether it says more than need be said. The other is whether it takes too many words to say it.

— *Mona Sheppard,* Plain Letters

9: How to Write Letters and Memos

Introduction

The first axiom for writing letters and memos — indeed, for writing *anything* — is this:

> **AXIOM ONE: Do not write without good reason.**

We're all being smothered in blizzards of paperwork. Some of it is necessary; unfortunately, much more of it is not. Make sure *your* writing doesn't fall into the second category.

Your priorities should go this way:

a. If you can *talk* your message in person, do it.

b. If you can't talk it in person, telephone.

c. If telephoning won't get the job done, *then,* and only, then, write.

Talking in person is quickest, least expensive, and least likely to lead to misunderstanding.

Talking by telephone is almost as quick, usually only slightly more expensive, and still gives the advantages of instant feedback.

Writing is by far the slowest method; it is also by far the most expensive. As we have said earlier, the average letter or memo these days costs at least $7.00, and often much more. So, if you must write, keep it short. Write as concisely and effectively as you can. Turn on the old gray matter; organize your thoughts. By spending a little extra time in the planning stage, you'll save much time later — for both yourself and your reader.

Plain Letters

Let me introduce you to a classic text on letterwriting: *Plain Letters*, by Mona Sheppard. You can get it for a little more than a dollar (actually, $1.10 as of September 1977) from the Superintendent of Documents, U.S. Government Printing Office, Washington, D. C. (Federal Stock Number 7610-205-1091.) It'll be one of your better investments, even though it cost only 35 cents when I first ran across this small masterpiece back in 1956. If government writers had been paying proper attention to Ms. Sheppard's excellent advice, their writing would be much better by now.

While you're waiting for your copy to arrive, I'll mention a few high points here:

Ms. Sheppard says "A good plain letter merits this 4-S badge of honor: *S*hortness, *S*implicity, *S*trength, and *S*incerity."

For *shortness,* Mona Sheppard says:
- Don't make a habit of repeating what is said in a letter in your answer.
- Avoid needless words and needless information.
- Beware of roundabout prepositional phrases, such as "with regards to" and "in reference to."
- Don't qualify your statements with irrelevant "ifs."

For *simplicity,* she says:
- Know your subject so well that you can discuss it naturally and confidently.
- Use short words, short sentences, and short paragraphs.
- Be compact. Don't separate related parts of sentences.
- Tie thoughts together so your reader can follow you from one to another without getting lost.

For *strength,* her "rules" are:
- Use specific, concrete words.
- Use more active verbs.
- Don't explain your answer before giving it. Give answers straightaway; then explain if necessary.
- Don't hedge. Avoid negative words.

Finally, for *sincerity,* Ms. Sheppard recommends:
- Be human. Use words that stand for human beings, like the names of persons and the personal pronouns *you, he, she, we* and so on.
- Admit mistakes. Don't hide behind meaningless words.
- Don't overwhelm your reader with intensives and emphatics.
- Don't be obsequious or arrogant. Strive to express yourself in a friendly way and with simple dignity befitting the United States Government. [Or your business, company, corporation, etc.]

Applying the 4-S formula

None of Ms. Sheppard's suggestions for clear letterwriting should come as a shock if you carefully study the rest of this handbook. Most of the principles she suggests have been discussed in some detail; what you have in the *Plain Letters* approach is a useful — and memorable — way of putting it all together.

Here are a few more of her suggestions for brevity and naturalness:

- Avoid stilted openings as "Reference is made to your letter." "This is in reply to your letter," and "We are in receipt of your letter."
- Refer to the inquiry by its date only, as "Thank you for your letter of June 10," or mention the subject of the inquiry in just enough words to let the reader know you understand what he had to say.
- Refer to the inquiry indirectly with a subordinate clause, as "The Craftsmanship of Lettering," *which you asked for in your letter of May 23,* is out of print.
- Don't describe an incoming letter as recent, particularly when the description doesn't fit. If you are embarrassed by the age of the inquiry, apologize for the delay in answering. For example, begin by saying, "We are sorry for the delay in answering your letter."

There are a few minor exceptions to this generally excellent advice. Let me mention a couple of them here:

If you are answering a Congressional inquiry, you'd probably better identify the original correspondence by both title and date in your opening paragraph. Many organizations and agencies require this, and it makes good sense, even though it appears to waste words.

Simply put, the reason is this: Senators and Congressmen (or, in actuality, their Administrative Aides) write literally scores, or even hundreds of letters every day and every week. They can't be expected to keep track of this correspondence or to remember it the way an individual would. You and I, for example, ordinarily write only a few letters and we know very well what we said in them.

So, if you can neatly apply Ms. Sheppard's advice to Congressional responses without breaking your organization's rules, fine. By all means do so. But take special care to make sure the correspondence you are answering can be readily identified.

Another important exception involves letters forwarded to you from another organization. When I was at NASA during the Apollo program, for example, letters written to the President were forwarded to us for answers. For a time we received hundreds or even thousands every week.

In such cases, the rule is simply this: explain that the letter — identified by subject and date —has been referred to you for an answer. State this politely and simply. Then get straight to the answer.

More advice on letter writing

Chairman Daniel O'Neal of the Interstate Commerce Commission (ICC) is one of the best friends of clear writing that I know. We need many more like him. In 1977, he issued a memo to the agency's Managing Director and to heads of ICC bureaus and offices. The title: "English—let's use it at the ICC."

The advice in the memo is so good I'd like to pass some of it along to you. With Chairman O'Neal's permission, here are some cogent excerpts:

> English is a remarkably clear, flexible, and useful language. We should use it in all of our communications.
>
> Commission correspondence is an important part of the face we turn to the world. Each letter we write creates a distinct impression of this agency in the mind of the reader. It also conveys, or fails to convey, information. Letters should be both *informational* and *understandable.*
>
> Although there has been general improvement in the quality of correspondence, I think it is worthwhile to lay a few ground rules for writing letters.
>
> First, a few thoughts on style and tone.
>
> Too often government writers fall back on the black sheep of the English family — Bureaucratese.
>
> ICC communications should be written in plain English with a simple vocabulary. One of the greatest writers of English, Winston Churchill, recommended the use of "short, simple words" and that remains good advice today.
>
> Convey your thoughts clearly. Use short, clear, declarative sentences. Use a noun, a verb, and an object of the verb when necessary. Use adjectives and adverbs only when they are essential to clear meaning.
>
> Don't get wrapped up in legal jargon that makes sense only to lawyers. Look at it from the reader's point of view. Take into account his probable understanding of the Commission and government in gen-

eral. Ask yourself, "If I had written this letter . . . what sort of response would I want?"

Above all, don't sound bureaucratic. Don't go through linguistic contortions to convey a simple thought . . .

Just speak normally. Be sure to avoid legalistic words or phrases such as *caveat, estopped,* or *viz.* Plain English will get the point across more effectively. And don't let the letter get bogged down with unnecessary details. Stick to the point. Irrelevant statements may indicate an extensive knowledge of the issue, but will probably confuse the reader.

The most common errors in the correspondence I have seen are dangling participles, split infinitives, and most of all, incorrect use of the plural pronoun. For example, the Southern Railroad is "it," not "them" or "they."

If the correspondent wants to know the status of a pending case, develop a reasonable estimated date of decision and give that date . . . Make sure the case meets the deadline . . .

Avoid defensive, self-serving, self-congratulatory statements . . . The correspondent will judge how well we do.

Also, in addition to making the letter understandable, try to make it personal. Let the reader know that a human is on the other end. Convey a warm tone.

Don't be afraid to break up a complex explanation of an issue with an occasional personal comment, just to remind the reader that a human is behind all those facts and figures. "I know this is a difficult situation . . . ," for example, might do in some cases where things look bad. "It's good to hear from you . . ." is appropriate when the correspondent has been helpful.

Letters needn't be puffy or flippant to be personal. They should simply let the reader know that somewhere in Washington, D.C., a human, not a computer, wrote that letter.

Avoid passing the buck. An individual should be referred to another federal agency only when absolutely necessary. We should refer the letter ourselves and tell the correspondent that we have done so. If we cannot provide the information, we should at least give a reason why.

Also, let's be willing to admit it when we make a mistake. We're not perfect . . .

One final point: The letters we write are for the benefit of the recipient, not the writer. Keep in mind that someone out there is waiting for the letter you are writing. Someone will have to make sense out of it. If it is hard to understand or if it wallows in a complex, bureaucratic double-talk, that individual's confidence in the government will drop a little bit more.

Remember that the person on the receiving end of a letter is our employer and we are explaining something about how the government — the citizens' tax money — is operating. It's not enough for a letter to be understood among ourselves.

A government letter writer should put himself in the shoes of the recipient and wonder whether somebody in Peoria or Spokane would really understand and be satisfied with a letter that starts, "Pursuant to Public Law 94-210 . . ."

Language is a mirror of thought. If our letters are rambling, twisted, and confusing, it's a pretty good bet that the thought behind them is that way too. And that is exactly how they are perceived by readers.

Let's show the American people that [fill in the name of your own organization here] speaks and writes plain English.

(signed) O'Neal

To all the above remarks, a heartfelt "Amen." (signed) Bates.

What Chairman O'Neal has written so eloquently does not apply just to the ICC, or even just to the government. Writers in private industry are advised to take a leaf from his book as well. The advice is excellent, and can be applied straight across the board.

The importance of tone

Every letter you write should have two purposes. The first is to accomplish an immediate objective, such as to convey information, to make a sale, or to ask for information. But your second purpose, although not so obvious, is also important: to build goodwill for yourself and your organization.

If you write in a way that angers or frustrates your reader, you will probably fail in *both* purposes. The effectiveness of your writing will be nil.

In general, tone in written communication is a lot like tact in personal relations — the more effective you are at it, the less likely it is to be noticed at all. If your technique becomes even slightly visible or conspicuous, chances are you had better go back and try again.

Guard against these common mistakes:

● Don't write in a way that angers or frustrates your reader.
● Don't insult the reader's intelligence.
● Don't say anything that might be construed as a putdown.
● Don't preach or pontificate; keep off the soapbox and out of the pulpit.
● Don't talk down to the reader.
● Don't write over the head of the reader.
● Don't use unsuitable humor or backslapping familiarity.
● Don't use sarcasm, exaggeration, or attempts at satire. The odds are

almost totally against you. You will almost inevitably be misunderstood or misconstrued by most of your readers.

● Don't make dogmatic, highly opinionated, aggressive, or smart-alecky pronouncements.

● Don't "argue" with the reader — that is, don't blatantly accuse the reader of being wrong, of having misunderstood, or of not being clear.

● Don't sound off at the reader.

● Don't write when you are angry; or if you do, tear up your letter, don't mail it!

● Don't pass the buck; if you have made a mistake, admit it.

Don't be obsequious or phony

Remember that you can lose points by going too far the other direction. Being overly obsequious, or buttering up the reader in an obvious way can be irritating, to say the least. Tact, courtesy, and sincerity — those are all good words, and good things to strive for. But be alert to how easy it is to step over the line toward submissiveness or insincerity.

Your letter represents not just you, but your organization or agency as well. You are responsible for doing your part to preserve its dignity. Don't whine, grovel, or get carried away with flowery words and honeyed phrases. And, don't make promises that cannot be kept.

The "you" attitude

Many government or corporate writers seem to believe they are justified in taking a cold, haughty, or detached approach toward members of the public. Not so. The writer is there to serve the public, not to hand down pronouncements from on high.

There is no reason not to use words that convey warmth, graciousness, and friendliness. Sometimes, though, you may feel you have a particularly difficult problem because of a boss's attitude. I've worked for people, and you probably have also, who put out orders against using the personal pronouns "I" and "we." (The prohibition against the "I" might pass muster. In many organizations, nobody but the top person is supposed to say "I." But the prohibition against "we" is misguided, in my opinion. Still, you'll just have to live with it.

Neither you nor I is likely to change the world — let alone the organization or the boss.)

Fortunately, there is a solution, and it's not so difficult as it may seem. Try the "you" approach. Instead of saying "We are . . ." and going into your sentence, simply recast it so that it starts with "you." Most of the time you'll find this works extremely well.

A few cautions are in order. There is danger in over-using "you." It is possible to overdo even a good thing. If your letter begins to sound phony, or appears to the reader to be overly altruistic — that is, if it creates a suspicion you are trying to put something over — it won't work. Suppose, for example, you are writing a letter of application. Your concern is for yourself, not your reader. In such cases, the "you" approach would be patently phony.

Here's a timeworn, but still apt, illustration of the point: "I've talked enough about my marvelous and incredible accomplishments. Now let's talk about *you*. What do *you* think about my marvelous and incredible accomplishments?"

Using "word softeners"

Avoid any inclination to use hardnosed expressions when something less offensive to the reader will get the message across just as well. Why say something such as "I have received your rotten letter in which you complained that . . . " when it is just as easy (and much more effective) to say, "I have received your letter concerning . . . "
You'll never find a better place to employ the golden rule. Put yourself in the reader's shoes. Sympathize. How would you like it if someone wrote to *you* that way?

Is tone always important?

It's true that tone is usually a factor in written communications, just as its counterpart, tone of voice, is important in oral communications. There are differences, however. If you are simply communicating run-of-the-mill information to persons you don't even know, or with whom your relationships are not close or delicate, you need not waste any extra attention on tone. Be polite and courteous, and that will be ample. To create the effect you desire, follow axiom two: slant your material to your reader. That means you must determine what relationship exists, or what relationship you desire to achieve. You must appraise both the reader and the situation you are writing about. With these things in mind, it should be relatively simple for you to choose appropriate words. The reader will "hear" them as you intend, without misunderstandings or hurt feelings.

Exercise: Faulty Tone

Sometimes my seminar students get carried away. The following exercise comes from real life. A student, trying to follow the principles of being concise and getting straight to the point, wrote this memo to his boss. Next day he brought it to class, a look of bewilderment on his face. Why was the boss so upset over a simple little memo?

Read what the student wrote and see if you can figure out what he did wrong. Then rewrite, with a more appropriate tone.

MEMO TO: John Joseph McBoss
FROM: Alexander Q. Subordinate

I must have your sign off immediately on the enclosed Personnel Handbook, which we received from Bob Otherguy for review before forwarding to Mr. Headman for final approval.

I intend to take no further action until I hear from you.

Suggested Rewrite

Bob Otherguy has sent us the enclosed Personnel Handbook for review. If it meets your approval, please sign your okay and send it back to me [maybe you said "Return it," that's okay] so I can forward it to Mr. Headman for final approval.

Axiom Two:

SLANT YOUR
PRESENTATION
TO YOUR
AUDIENCE

Let us treat men and women well;
Treat them as if they were real;
Perhaps they are.

— Ralph Waldo Emerson (1803-1882)

10: Know your Audience

Introduction

To communicate, you must aim your message directly at your audience. To do this you must (a) know as much as possible about the *make-up* of your audience; and (b) know as much as possible about the *interests* of that audience.

Regardless of what your message may be, you can't expect to deliver it successfully if you always use the same approach, paying no attention to the differences in background of your various readers. What works extremely well for communicating with one group may not work at all for another. To make the problem more difficult, the reasons for the differences may not be at all obvious.

I have used the term "audience" here advisedly. It's true that the word is usually reserved for listeners attending oral presentations. But that's narrowing the term unduly; as used here, it's intended to be a synonym for *readers,* not simply listeners. And, since readers — unlike listeners — do not give you instant feedback, it becomes all the more important that you size up your audience in advance.

AXIOM TWO: Slant your presentation for your audience.

An audience is comprised of individuals with different backgrounds and personalities, and each of those members is likely to hear or read your message in a different way. Don't be taken in by the fact that the word "audience" is a collective noun that takes a singular form of the verb. This is just a quirk of grammar. An audience can be construed as being either singular or plural, and you can be quite sure that an audience of more than one person will seldom if ever react as a single entity. You can transmit a message you believe to be unmistakably clear, and yet various members of the audience will "hear" very different things — perhaps some of them will come up with diametrically opposite interpretations.

Why is this so? Simple — each individual represents the sum total of a lifetime of "perceived reality," and that "perceived reality" can never be the same for any two persons. Thus, one individual shares a message with another to a limited extent only — namely, the congruent area of "perceived reality" that the two individuals have in common. Does that explanation sound far out? Well, if I'm confusing you, take comfort in the fact that I'm confusing myself too.

To bring theory back down to earth, what I do know is that when a writer uses words or ideas alien to the reader's knowledge and experience, there are inevitably some gaps in the communication. And, the harder the writer may try to bridge the gaps, the more likely that for some of the audience the message may become distorted or bent totally out of shape.

Checklist for audience analysis

Fortunately, there are many things you can usually find out in advance, and if you take the composite results, you are much more likely to send a "receivable" message. The following checklist items are not necessarily in order of importance, but you will want to get answers to as many of them as you can. Here's what you need to find out:

- Age (or range of ages)
- Sex (or percentages of each)
- Occupation(s) represented
- Educational background (average years of schooling completed, types of studies, majors, etc.)
- Level of experience

NOTE: Even though the concern here is written *communication, I have used the same audience analysis checklist most speechwriters use. Much of what I've learned about analyzing audiences comes from speechwriting — the best training, and the toughest school, for learning how different audiences respond. If a speech gets off on the wrong foot, you find out very quickly — the hard way. Feedback from the audience may take many different forms. If you're lucky, you'll get off with scowls or sullen expressions. If you're not so lucky, it can be anything from heckling and jeers to the launching of over-ripe fruit.*

Age

This is usually fairly easy to find out. For purposes of simplicity, let's stick to the speechwriting analogy, even though most of your writing will probably be directed to readers rather than to listeners. In either event, you are probably going to know whether you are writing for, say, grade school, high school, or college age people; or, perhaps, members of the Junior Chamber of Commerce (relatively young), the Rotary Club (probably somewhat older), or the Association of Retired Employees (senior citizens, to use the current euphemism).

Sex

You can probably find out whether you are writing for an all-male audience, an all-female audience, or a mixture of both. Some years ago I wrote a speech intended for an audience of electronics engineers. Then, at just about the last possible second, I discovered that the occasion was to be a dinner meeting, and that the engineers' wives would be there too. In the revised version, done in total panic on an airplane enroute to Chicago, many of the points of the speech remained essentially the same, but the overall approach had to be changed drastically.

Occupation

Obviously you would write quite differently for a group of electronics engineers than you would for a group of sociologists or an association of retail merchants. There's no need to labor this point.

Educational Background

Remember that education and occupation are the items that separate otherwise similar persons into what sociologists call "subcultures." People with major differences in those two important areas are often likely to have little in common; they may find it difficult to communicate with one another at an abstract level. In writing for disparate groups, keep in mind the importance of concrete words that have meaning in terms of the senses: seeing, hearing, smelling, touching, and tasting. Other, more abstract words may mean one thing to members of one subculture, and something entirely different to members of a different subculture. Look out especially when you use slang terms. Slang changes so fast that by the time one group newly discovers it, the group that originated it has probably already discarded it. As a member of the older generation, there was a period when I had trouble understanding the language of my teen-age children — until fortunately, either they or I, or perhaps all of us, grew out of it.

Level of Experience

Once more you must be analytical. You must try to deduce what your audience already knows or understands about your subject. Anticipate as well as you can what additional information the reader(s) will need or want to have.

Analyzing Your Reader(s)

Okay, let's stop talking about speechwriting and turn to written communications such as letters and memos. Let's take a hypothetical case in which someone has written you a letter, and you are responding.

Your first clues — indeed, virtually the only ones — will undoubtedly come from the letter you've received. Read it carefully, looking for every clue you can find.

What kind of paper is it written on? Embossed stationery? A piece of lined paper torn from a tablet? A business letterhead? If the latter, does it indicate the person's organization, business, or other affiliation? Is the writer's title indicated?

Is the letter handwritten or typewritten? How well are the ideas expressed? How about the vocabulary? The spelling? All these items can help add up to an overall impression.

The "age" question may or may not be answered, but you can probably tell whether a letter has been written by a young student, on the one hand, or by an adult, on the other. The "sex" question can usually, but not always, be answered by the person's name and title, or there may be other indications.

The occupation or profession is often self-evident, or at least easy to figure out: business executive? farmer? physician? and so on.

Suppose some or all of these questions remain unanswered even after your best analytical detective work. What do you do then?

Writing for the "Average" Reader

Is there such a thing as an "average" reader? Probably not, but many times you'll have to write as if there is. Essentially, what you must do is to write for the "least common denominator."

That doesn't mean you must "write down" or condescend. Heaven forbid. It does mean you must choose your words and thoughts so they will have appeal to beginners *and* old hands, tyros *and* experts, young *and* old, and all the other possible permutations. Picture an imaginary reader in your mind — a reader who is reasonably intelligent, but not necessarily schooled; a reader who has good common sense but probably doesn't have a specialized background in the subject you are discussing. The clearer that mental picture, the better you will write.

Okay, take it from there. This means you'll *use simple words, weeding out technical shoptalk and jargon* — or you'll explain such language if you feel you must use it for accuracy of expression. You will *start on common ground,* choosing as a beginning something that your reader probably knows about. You will *progress one step at a time* to the more difficult material. You will *be as logical and clear as you possibly can.* And you will strive to *"slant" the material so it will be as interesting and understandable as you can make it.*

Al Lefcowitz, in his excellent *Writer's Handbook,* puts it this way: " . . .*shape the expression to fit the thought. That is, the audience should not have to struggle through language more complex than the situation requires.*"

Axiom Three:

*"Hell", said the Duchess, "Let
go my leg!"*

—Traditional "Narrative Hook"

11: Getting and Holding the Reader's Attention

Introduction

Effective writing must be something more than just well-conceived ideas clearly expressed. Important as these qualities are, they aren't the be-all and end-all. There is another necessary ingredient: the writer must win the reader's attention and interest, or there is no real meeting of the minds.

A generation ago, students of the short story were constantly drilled to employ the device known to the trade as the "narrative hook." The example at the top of this page is a humorous demonstration of how to do it. As an attention getter, that famous line is supposed to combine a number of things of great interest to the average reader: *excitement,* portrayed by the mildly profane "Hell," chosen instead of other Anglo-Saxon monosyllables that would have been more shocking to the average reader in those euphemistic days of my youth; *royalty,* personified by the Duchess; and *sex, violence,* and *action* — summed up neatly in the "Let go my leg!"

Short stories today are an anachronism; hardly anyone writes them any more. The form has become almost as defunct as that of the Petrarchan Sonnet. How many of either have you run across lately?

But the short story form lives on — slightly disguised but nonetheless recognizable, in today's prime time television "action" shows. Just watch a few of them as they come on; later that night you can compare their openings with those of the late, late shows — movies filmed in the '30s and '40s. You'll quickly see an object lesson.

The very popular "Kojak" show, for example, would never start out with an old-fashioned, long and rambling narrative: "In the city of New York, during the winter of 1976, there was a horrifying series of events that. . ." And so on.

Not on your life. The show always starts right out with the most exciting action sequence that can be plucked out of the entire hour. The opening grabber will undoubtedly be some very different actions from one week to the next: one time it may be someone being punched in the nose; in the next episode, a victim may be thrown off Brooklyn Bridge. But whatever it is, you can lay odds that it will be the most exciting and dramatic moment the writers can dredge up from anywhere in the full-hour script.

Most writers don't call this technique the "narrative hook" any more. More likely they'll call it a teaser or a grabber. But whatever they call it, it has but one purpose — to grab the viewer's attention, instantly. That is the moment when the network shows are all changing at once; viewers are reaching for their channel selectors to twist quickly through each program until they find something that interests them. The sponsors don't intend for those potential viewers to be put off by seeing a long list of titles and credits; they know that if that is what is going on, the viewers are going to continue twisting to another channel. Chances are, they will make sure to hook you, and all other potential viewers, by not "rolling the credits" until perhaps as long as five or six minutes into the action.

Compare this approach with that of a movie coming on the late, late show — one that was not originally filmed for television. You'll observe that the opening credits are likely to keep rolling for several minutes or more.

The pace is leisurely; you'll see the name of the producer, then, perhaps, the logo or trademark of the studio. Observe how long MGM's Leo keeps yawning (hope this mental image isn't contagious), before they even get around to letting you know the name of the picture. Notice the elapsed time as they scroll down the credits: the producer, the directors, all the stars, great and small — some of the really big ones listed as "Mr." or "Miss" — followed by the supporting players, the bit players, the camera and sound men, the script girls, the grips, and so on ad infinitum. Perhaps, in very small print, they'll eventually even show you the name of the writer. Or, in bigger print, the name of the producer's brother-in-law who was given all the credit.

The audiences those movies were made for had traveled — perhaps for miles — to get to the theater. What's more important, they had bought tickets at the box office and paid their way in. They were definitely a captive group. There wasn't any danger they'd change channels for a more exciting show.

Well, there's a great deal more competition for the viewer's attention these days. That's why everyone goes to so much trouble to introduce some interest and excitement right up front.

Notice what they do next. Once they've captured that attention, they can start going back, picking up earlier details, filling in the background, explaining what has gone before and how it all fits together.

That's not a bad trick for all writers to remember, all the time. We live in a media-dominated age. Audiences aren't nearly so patient as they used to be. If we intend to capture their attention, we'd better do our best to get to our point quickly, without any fooling around.

How many letters have crossed your desk in recent weeks that you had to read several times before you could even begin to figure out what the writer was driving at? Chances are, quite a few.

Did you have to fight your way through rambling introductions, extraneous material, and unnecessary background information before the writer actually got down to the main business?

If those letters were TV shows, you undoubtedly would have tuned them out. Since they were probably important to you, you fought your way through them, wasting your valuable time and perhaps never finding out exactly what you wanted to know.

Engrave this in big, bold letters on the tablets of your memory: *The reader has a right to know, as early on as possible, what a communication is about. Write so that your reader can get the message quickly — on the very first reading.*

AXIOM THREE. Get straight to the point.

Here's a step-by-step analysis of how to do it:

1. Formulate a simple, one-sentence statement of what the writing is all about. Do this before you actually begin to write.

2. Write down your statement of purpose. Phrase it so it will make the reader interested in continuing to read. The best way to do this is to put yourself in the reader's shoes, and figure out what would be important to you in such a case. In the process, ask yourself the following questions:

      a. What is the *real* reason I am writing this?
      b. What is the *main idea* I intend to convey?
      c. What *response* do I desire to elicit from the reader?

3. Set forth the points most interesting or important to the reader at the very beginning. (These may not be the same points as those of most interest to you. Don't think of your own preferences at all; put the reader first.)

4. Put the conclusion, or its equivalent, near the beginning — perhaps not in the very first paragraph, but certainly as close to it as you can manage. Remember that you're not writing a detective story in which you hold things back from the reader. Do just the opposite of that: give the answers the reader needs without trying for a build-up of suspense.

5. Use the "flashback" technique to fill in the details. Make your reader have full understanding by furnishing the background, the ancient history, or whatever it takes to explain and support your case.

Here's a good example of a memo that's straight to the point, with no "flashback" needed. The sender and receiver were both thoroughly familiar with the problem under discussion:

The White House

To: John Dean
From: Charles Colson

Now what the hell do I do?

Exercise: Getting straight to the point

This is an actual announcement, copied from an original posted on the company bulletin board. "Only the names have been changed, to protect the innocent." Please read this announcement carefully several times before you answer the questions that follow it.

ANNOUNCEMENT

SUBJECT: Meeting on "Management by Objective," December 10-12.

1. On December 10-12 the Corporation will host a conference on Management by Objective which will be held in the Building Six Auditorium.
2. Approximately 300 conference participants are expected, which will cause crowding at some of the Corporation's facilities. The Building Six Parking Lot will be reserved for conference attendees. Employees who normally work there should make an effort to use other lots. Also, between 11:30 a.m. and 12:30 p.m., the Administrative Building Cafeteria No. 3 will be occupied by conference attendees. Corporation employees should plan accordingly.
3. As always your cooperation in these matters is greatly appreciated.

Now answer these questions:
1. Does the subject line *really* tell the reader what the announcement is all about?
2. If you were a corporation employee reading the announcement on the company bulletin board, would you — after reading paragraph 1 — get the impression that you were being invited to attend the conference?
3. After careful reading, what do you believe are the two *real* messages the announcement is intended to convey?

When you've answered these three questions, rewrite the announcement, reorganizing and restructuring it. Put first things first. Start with the subject line itself. (Hint: Do you need a "To" line? That is, should this announcement be addressed to *all* corporation employees? Or is it really addressed to just a portion of those employees? Think about it.)

Please don't look at the suggested rewrite until you have completed your own version. There's a very good chance yours might be better.

Suggested Rewrite for Exercise: Getting Straight to the Point

ANNOUNCEMENT

TO: All Employees Who Park on the Building Six Parking Lot
     All Employees Who Eat in Cafeteria No. 3

SUBJECT: Parking Restrictions on Building Six Parking Lot — Dec. 10, 11, and 12.
     Eating Restrictions in Cafeteria No. 3 — 11:30 a.m. 12:30 p.m., same dates

1. Please use other parking lot and cafeteria facilities during the time periods indicated in the subject line.

2. We ask you to cooperate in observing these restrictions because the Corporation is hosting a conference on "Management by Objective," December 10, 11, and 12, in the Building Six Auditorium. We expect to accommodate about 300 conference participants from other organizations. As hosts, we must reserve facilities for them.

3. We're sorry about the inconvenience, but your cooperation will help us make the conference run smoothly. We appreciate it very much.

Exceptions to the rule

Are there ever cases when it would be better *not* to get straight to the point? Well, there are exceptions to just about everything, and this one is no exception.

Suppose you have to tell the reader some bad news, or turn down a request. In that case you will want to break it gently; cushion the blow, as it were. If you can, start with some kind of good news first, or at least seek a common ground with the reader. Be human, and humane.

But the bad news is still there, and you can't avoid it indefinitely. So, cushion the blow — but then, *get to the point.* Express regret or sympathy if you can, but don't apologize. Remember that you do no kindness by keeping the reader in suspense unnecessarily. And you do an actual *un*kindness if you hold out hopes that you might change your mind. (This subject is discussed in more detail in the chapter on letter writing.)

When all else fails, read the instructions.
— Ancient adage

In case of fire, stand in the hall and
shout "Fire!"
— The Kidner Report

12: How To Do "How-To-Do-Its"

Introduction

Instructions should be simple, direct, concise, clear, and *precise.* All these virtues are important enough in any kind of writing, but in doing "how-to-do-its" they are absolutely essential.

This chapter is chiefly about techniques for writing *instructions,* but most of the information given here can be carried over to the closely related areas of writing *rules* and *regulations,* discussed in the next chapter.

In this area, your most important axiom is:

AXIOM FOUR: Show the reader!

Try to anticipate all problems, and make sure you deal with each one — simply, logically, and *in the right order.* I could give you examples of how *not* to do it that would (apologies to my friend and colleague Ralph Gibson) "bring a suspicion of moisture to your steely-blue eyes."

Let's look at a typical example. Some time ago, I bought an electronic ignition system for my car. An inscription on the top of the box said the device would be easy to install — "Just follow the simple instructions." Does that sound familiar?

When I opened the box, I was happy to see that the instructions were spelled out step by step — a good sign. That's the best way to write instructions. I immediately began to feel a false sense of security.

I noticed something else. The manufacturers wanted to make sure I wouldn't lose the instructions, so they had glued the instruction sheet on the back of the ignition module. Great!

As I recall, the first step went something like this: "*Step One. Using the ignition module as a template, drill two 3/8-inch holes at a suitable spot in the engine compartment. Using two 3/8-inch sheetmetal screws, mount unit firmly to chassis.*"

Well, that sounds clear enough, except for the "suitable spot," and I suppose a reasonably bright person could figure that out. So what's the complaint? Surely I don't have to remind you that the instructions were glued on the *back* of the module!

As I say, that sort of mistake is typical. Even though the instructions were well-written in many respects, putting the steps in the wrong order is a most serious offense. As discussed elsewhere, you can choose from many methods of development, but in writing instructions, the *sequential* or *chronological* method usually works best. Why? Because instructions usually must be followed in an established sequence. Thus, one of the worst crimes a writer can commit is to present steps out of sequence. Confusion could lead to damaging equipment or to injuring or killing an operator.

Checklist for writing instructions

1. Use short sentences and short paragraphs. Numbered sequences are usually best.
2. Arrange in logical order. (I know you are tired of hearing it, but we *must* get this in the checklist.)
3. Make your statements specific. (Once more I'll remind you of the Kipling jingle: Who-What-Where-When-Why-How, not necessarily in that order.)
4. Use the *imperative mood.* Definition: The imperative mood is a form used to indicate command, wish, or permission. Examples: "Get out of

here!" "Go to your room at once." "Set the dial pointer at 180 on the scale."

5. Put the most important item in each sentence at the beginning.

6. Say one thing in each sentence. Don't try to pack in any extra information or thoughts beyond what it takes to do the job. Let's repeat — say *one thing only* in each sentence.

7. Choose your words carefully. Avoid *jargon* and technical terms if you can, by using everyday words familiar to the average reader. If you *must* use technical terms, define them. One good way to do this is to furnish the reader with a glossary of technical terms.

8. Give an example or an *analogy,* if you feel a statement may puzzle the reader. (Using properly captioned diagrams or illustrations is often even better.)

9. Check your completed draft for logic of presentation. Make sure you have progressed from (a) the known to the unknown; or (b) from the general to the specific.

10. Don't omit steps or take shortcuts, in the belief that something is obvious, and the reader will understand. Murphy's Law promises us that the reader will *misunderstand* if such a thing is at all possible, and probably will even if it's *not* possible.

How to describe simultaneous operations

Sometimes you may have to describe two or more steps that must be performed at the same time. Here are a couple of suggestions on ways of handling these toughies: (a) Write an introductory paragraph of explanation *before* you start on the actual step-by-step procedures; (b) include *both* steps in the same numbered item, with a large-print NOTICE that they must be performed together; *or* (c) use a *double-column layout* to indicate the simultaneous operations. Take special care not to overload any of the numbered steps with irrelevant detail.

Exercises:
An exercise on how to write instructions can be found in Part Three, page 202.

Axiom Four:

Any member introducing a dog into the Society's premises shall be liable to a fine of one pound. Any animal leading a blind person shall be deemed to be a cat.
— *Rule 46, Oxford Union Society, London*

There are two things wrong with almost all legal writing. One is its style. The other is its content.
— *Fred Rodell (retired Yale law professor)*

13: How to Write Regulations

Introduction

Writing is far from being an exact science, as we have said. Even when we try our best to be precise, we fail more often than not. Readers come up with interpretations totally different from those we intend to convey.

Law is, if anything, even less exact. After all, laws and regulations are made up of words; they can be no more precise than their ingredients. No law has ever been written that didn't have an exception — sometimes many more than one.

It's an age-old problem. How can you write something clearly, so that it is easy to understand, without oversimplifying? How do you keep from losing or changing important shades of meaning? It's hard enough with any kind of writing. But when you deal with laws and regulations the problems become much more serious. Laws usually affect lives and pocketbooks, and you can't get much more serious than that.

But good things are happening.

In New York State in 1977, an assemblyman named Sullivan sponsored a revolutionary "Plain Language" bill that was signed into law (after much hassling and an amendment or two) to take effect in the fall of 1978.

The new law is now being used as a model by a number of other states drafting similar laws. It requires leases and other consumer documents to be written in "a clear and coherent manner using words with common everyday meanings." A few years ago these kinds of laws were unheard of. Now they're growing fast. Progress, it's wonderful!

Several years ago the state of Pennsylvania put into effect a regulation requiring auto-insurance policies to rate at least 40 on the Flesch Readability Scale. (See *readability* entry in the handbook section.)

Time magazine says several other states have legislated plain language requirements for health and accident policies. The recently enacted Federal Pension Reform Act requires that company booklets be written "in a manner calculated to be understood by the average participant." And, says *Time,* the new Federal Warranty Law states that product warranties have to be "simple and readily understood."

But most legal documents and government regulations continue to be written in difficult, obscure, and ambiguous language. We've come a long way, baby, but we still have a long way to go.

Check with the legal staff

Unless you are trained in the law, take this advice: check out every word of every regulation you write with the organization's legal staff. This can be good or bad — it's up to you. I know many writers who hate every minute of it. They bypass getting legal coordination every time they can. Frankly, that isn't very bright. More than once a lawyer has saved me from a severe attack of the stupids.

Be glad you have a lawyer to check everything out. You need not have an adversary relationship. After all, you are both on the same side, and if you're not you should be. You can argue over words, phrases, meanings, and intents all day — and still be friends.

Mutual respect is the key. Your relationship is — or should be — symbiotic. Each of you has special knowledge to contribute to the accuracy of the end product, and working together will increase that accuracy. Both of you should have the courage of your convictions, but should be willing to bend a little to achieve the desired goal.

Don't permit yourself to be snowed by legal erudition. Some lawyers know the law inside out, but still write the most convoluted prose imaginable. Maybe they know *too* much. Balance things out by injecting a mixture of common sense and freely admitted ignorance. If the lawyer can explain things to you, you can in turn explain them to the public.

Much bad legal and regulatory writing stems simply from custom and habit. The old story — you're as tired of hearing it as I am of telling it: "We've always done it that way."

But that isn't the whole problem. Much legal writing is as miserable as it is simply because the writers don't know how to do any better.

Some steps in the right direction

Jim Miner, chairman of the American Bar Association's Committee on Legal Drafting, is a man I greatly admire. Maybe some day, if I'm lucky, I'll get a chance to sit in on one of his famous seminars. Friends of mine who have been through his drill tell me he's a marvel.

Miner explains that previous regulations are almost guaranteed to be written in gobbledygook. He says that only the worst sections of any regulation are ever handed down and used over and over again in subsequent writing. These obscurely written passages are preserved, he explains, because only the most incomprehensible sections of any regulation or law are litigated in court. "The language has been tested," says Miner, "because it is so bad that no one could understand it."

He points out that arguments can be long and bloody, but once a decision has been reached, the words "blessed" by the judge's decision go into the form books for other regulation writers to use.

I particularly enjoy the following paragraph, which Miner distributes to all his classes as a typical example of what's wrong with most legal writing:

We respectfully petition, request and entreat, that due and adequate provision be made, this day and the date hereinafter subscribed, for the satisfying of this petitioner's nutritional requirements and for the organizing of such methods as may be deemed necessary and proper to assure the reception by and for said petitioner of such quantities of baked cereal products as shall, in the judgment of the aforementioned petitioners constitute a sufficient supply thereof.

In case you don't recognize this legalistic version of an extremely familiar passage, it translates to "Give us this day our daily bread."

Cutting out the legalistic jargon

One step to improve legal writing is a simple one: substitute everyday words for "legalisms." Obviously, we can't list them all, but here's a sampling of some of the worst offenders with suggestions for replacing them. Here goes:

abeyance. Try *wait,* or *postpone action.*

accompanied by. Most of the time you can substitute *with.*

affix your signature. Just say *sign the paper.*

afford an opportunity. How about *allow?* Or *permit?*

as of this day. That's saying *today* the hard way.

at an early date. Try substituting *soon.*

at your earliest convenience. What if your reader doesn't find it convenient at all? For best results, be as specific as you can.

claim. Try *say, charge, contend,* or (rarely) *allege. (Watch your tone. Allege* can be dynamite.)

cognizance. Mona Sheppard says: "Avoid this big word both in its legal meaning of jurisdiction and in its common meaning of *heed* or *notice.* Instead of saying *under the cognizance of this office,* be specific, as *this office does not audit travel vouchers.*

e.g. This abbreviation stands for the Latin *exempli gratia,* which means *for example.* Many readers don't know what it means. Avoid confusion. Simply write *for example.*

earliest practicable date. Say *as soon as possible.*

eschew. This means *give up.* Most of the time that's what you should write. But you need not always eschew *eschew.* Sometimes it's useful — it was good enough for Mark Twain, and that's pretty good. Also, Richard Wincor, a lawyer who writes wisely, wittily, and well, defends the word. He goes on to say that " . . . rare words should be used only once in a long while. Whoever uses them sparingly appears reliable, but with hidden depths."

endeavor to ascertain. That's the longwinded way of saying *try to find out.*

finalize. This miserable abomination of a word is on the forbidden list of most careful writers, but it continues to crop up anyway. Why not substitude *end, conclude, finish,* or *complete?*

fullest possible extent. Try substituting something like *as much as you* (or somebody) *can,* or — better — leave it out entirely. Mona Sheppard calls it meaningless padding.

hereby. Some lawyers appear to love this word almost more than life itself. Too bad, because it is a real confuser. Sometimes it means *by means of this,* but you can't tell what the *this* is referring to. It could be an entire document, or a part of it, or at a particular moment, but perhaps a little later. You see, it has no definite or fixed position in space or in time. Forget it. Unless you just want to sound fancy and legal, you'd better *eschew* it.

herein/herewith. It won't do much good to define these words, because the meanings are not difficult. Unfortunately, they can often lead to unsuspected ambiguity. Most of the time you'll make your writing clearer by leaving them out.

hereinafter. This little word, unlike the others in this list, probably deserves a medal. It is a time and space saver, particularly useful for setting up abbreviated names to be used throughout the remainder of a legal document.

i.e. This is an abbreviation for the Latin *id est.* As with *e.g. (with* which it is sometimes confused) many readers simply don't know what it means. Say *that is,* and avoid misunderstanding.

implement. What would the government do without this word? I don't know, but it would be interesting to find out. The word simply means *carry out* or *put into effect.* Unfortunately, saying it that simply doesn't sound nearly impressive enough to suit many writers.

in compliance with your request. Say *as requested.*

interpose no objection. How about *I do not object,* or *I approve.*

objective. Try *aim* or *goal.*

obligate. Frankly, I know that the budget and fiscal people won't give up on this one without a struggle, but sometimes *bind* will work. Not always.

obligation can be *debt.*

over the signature of. Why not just say *signed by?*

preclude. You could substitute *shut out* or *prevent.* But I don't always preclude *preclude,* so I shouldn't expect you to.

promulgate. Some people would rather promulgate than eat. We are going to have a rough time stamping this one out, but we can try. A good substitute is *issue.* Sometimes *publish* will work.

pursuant. Old-line members of the military services would probably go up in smoke if they couldn't say *Pursuant to the authority contained in* whatever it is. Just for kicks, I wish they would at least occasionally replace it with *under.*

secure. This is another word that has built-in ambiguity. The military services use *secure* in a specialized way; they are not about to change, and I don't suppose they should. But the rest of us should bypass *secure* by saying *get, take,* or *obtain.*

since. This word is often misused, and I must admit with shame that I'm frequently among the guilty. *Since,* in its primary meaning, should carry the idea of *from then until now,* or *from some particular time in the past and on up to the present.* But many writers use it regularly as a substitute for *because,* with resulting confusion to the reader.

subsequent to means *after*.

terminated. Let's terminate *terminated*. Say *ended* — it's just as final and much neater.

telephonically. This is a real monstrosity. I am horrified to learn that there are agencies that won't permit their employees to write or say *by telephone*. They must think they are impressing somebody, but all I know is that they are *de*pressing me.

utilize. Writers often utilize *utilize* when they should use *use*. (A tip of the hat to Bill Gilbert, Public Affairs Officer of the D.C. Council of Governments, from whom I "borrowed" this definition.)

verification. Sometimes you can at least unsmother the verb and say *verify* or *verified*. Other times you can simply say *proof*.

whereas. This is a real troublemaker of a word. It doesn't really mean much of anything. Still, some lawyers love to fling it around — I suppose they think it adds a legalistic overtone to an otherwise mundane and unexceptional document. Sometimes they use it to mean *since*, or *considering that*. Other times it means *while on the contrary*. Most of the time it doesn't really mean much of anything. Still, I don't suppose a Presidential Proclamation would be considered authentic without a nice *whereas* at the beginning of each paragraph.

One last offense has been saved for special mention: *and/or*. This inseparable pair is greatly disliked by many writers, including the impeccable E.B. White. But Richard Wincor, writing from the viewpoint of the law, calls *and/or* "an essential barbarism." His implication is that the expression has its uses. I agree. At least once or twice in this book you can catch me using it. Nevertheless, I would suggest that there are *usually* ways of writing around it, and by avoiding the expression whenever you can, you will certainly improve the accuracy of your prose.

Exercise: Rewriting a Legal Document

Here is the actual language of the old personal-loan note of the First National City Bank. Rewrite it as simply and clearly as you can, but be careful not to change any legal meanings. This is a difficult assignment, but just consider it a challenge! When you have finished, you'll have a chance to compare your version with the actual new version now in use. The First National City Bank's own editorial and legal staff accepted the challenge and managed to do a marvelously clear rewrite. You'll find it below.

"In the event of default in the payment of this or any other Obligation or the performance or observance of any term or other contract of agreement evidencing or relating to any Obligation or any Collateral on the Borrower's part to be performed or observed; or the undersigned Borrower shall die; or any of the undersigned become insolvent or make an assignment for the benefit of creditors; or a petition shall be filed by or against any of the undersigned under any provision of the Bankruptcy Act; or any money, securities or property of the undersigned now or hereafter on deposit with or in the possession of or under the control of the Bank shall be attached or become subject to distraint proceedings or any order or process of any court . . . "

Suggested Rewrite of Exercise: Rewriting a Legal Document

I truly didn't expect you to perform any miracles on this, since you were working with limited information. If you came up with something even remotely like the following, you did well. This is the way the Bank staff did it:

I'll be in default:

1. If I don't pay an installment on time; or
2. If any other creditor tries by legal process to take any money of mine in your possession.

The rules for shall and will

Thirty years ago, traditional grammarians were still quite concerned about the differences between *shall* and *will*. In those days, the formal rule was that, to express simple futurity, you would use *shall* in the first person, and *will* in the second and third persons. That is, *I shall, you will, he/she/it will,* etc.

To express determination, promise, or intention, it was the other way around: *will* for first person; *shall* for second and third persons.

Most of those distinctions have just about disappeared in recent years. *Will* is generally considered acceptable in informal usages for all purposes, and nobody will raise an eyebrow.

When it comes to the language of regulation, however, the old rules still apply. In such cases, of course, your primary concern will be the usages for second and third person, not first. For example, if you write "The contractor will furnish . . ." you are implying simple futurity only, and there is no binding force. But "The contractor *shall* furnish" means that the contractor is under firm direction to perform.

The rules for **must** and **should**

In the language of regulations, the word *must* is used as an imperative to indicate a necessity, a binding force. The word *should* carries the idea of obligation, but not of necessity. It is, accordingly, a weaker word.

Checklist for writing regulations

1. State the purpose of the regulation as simply, briefly, and clearly as you possibly can.

2. Tell who will be governed by the regulation. Be specific.

3. Use short sentences and plain words. *Define your terms.*

4. Prefer the present tense whenever possible.

5. Use the *imperative mood.*

6. Put the most important things first. Start with the known and move to the unknown. Start with the general and move to the specific — *logically.*

7. Say one thing, and only one thing, in each sentence.

8. If there is an exception, put it in the very next sentence.

9. Check your completed draft for possible ambiguity. If necessary, *rewrite, rewrite, rewrite.*

10. Don't omit any steps or take any shortcuts. Spell everything out, all the way.

NOTE: The legal department of your organization will probably give you a hard time on items 7 and 8. You may lose. But don't give up without a struggle. These two items are highly important. It is a mistaken notion to think that all qualifications, all exceptions, and the like must be packaged within a single set of periods. You will often be told that you must do it this way — to keep people from taking information out of context and twisting it. Don't believe it. A number of excellent lawyers have assured me that this simply is not so. In fact, they say that overpacked sentences can well lead to problems and litigation. Trying to fit too many ideas into one long, complicated sentence will often result in total incomprehensibility — not just to the lay reader, but often to the lawyers as well.

Exception Disclosures

Because courts have ruled that regulations have the same force and effect as law, it is well to include in most regulations an "exception disclosure," such as "Exceptions to the provisions of this regulation may be made only by [fill in organization title.] Send requests for exceptions to [organization title.]"

Consistency

Let me bring this chapter on writing regulations to an end by reminding you once more to be consistent. Do *not* use different words to denote the same thing. Do *not* use the same word to denote different things. Set a style, choose a vocabulary, and stick with it. In other types of writing, you can commit these "sins" and perhaps even get away with some of them. When you are writing regulations, you cannot. Engrave this next axiom on the tablets of your memory:

AXIOM FIVE. Be consistent.

Axiom Five:

*I never understand anything
until I have written about it.*

—E.M. Forster

14: How to Write Reports

Why the old-fashioned outline often doesn't work

We've all been brainwashed. Back in high school, our English teachers said, "Always make an outline before writing." And we believe them still. Why, then, do most writers hate outlines so?

Mostly, because we know in our hearts that the way we were taught to outline often doesn't work.

Why not?

Let's compare our experiences—mine is probably similar to yours: when my teacher assigned an outline to be turned in, corrected, and then followed by a composition, I always wrote the composition first. Then I worked backwards and made the outline. I was close-mouthed and cagey about my method; indeed, I believed I was the only one who used it. Years later, in graduate school, I confessed my "crime" to some fellow English majors; their sheepish admissions gave me the first inkling that hosts of others secretly defy the sacrosanct outline system.

Chances are, our teachers did too. All evidence points in that direction. I know now that most working writers make only the sketchiest of outlines before beginning a short assignment, and not much more before a long one—totally unlike the picayunishly specific blueprints English teachers require of their students.

Writers with practical experience learn the hard way that one idea grows out of another, one sentence out of another, one paragraph out of another. Almost always, a formal outline constructed in massive detail at the beginning will bear only faint resemblance to the ultimate product.

But, as I said earlier, we've been brainwashed—told we must *always* prepare a full outline according to the timeworn tradition; first, a Roman numeral, then a capital letter, then an Arabic numeral, a lower case letter, and so on. Unfortunately, the whole routine is usually an exercise in futility. How can anyone realistically outline in advance every detail of a projected piece of writing? During the actual creative process, writing the very first paragraph may alter the writer's entire outlook—and outline.

What, never? Well, hardly ever!

Every principle in this book—even this one—has exceptions. Some scientific and technical reports are virtually straitjacketed as to format; they almost always must have an ABSTRACT, a FOREWORD, an INTRODUCTION, a DISCUSSION, a SUMMARY (often with RECOMMENDATIONS), and frequently an APPENDIX and a BIBLIOGRAPHY To the extent that your report must conform to this pattern, you have, in a manner of speaking, an "outline." Beyond that, your organization may have a traditional format you must follow in developing ideas and presenting factual material.

These are "givens." What you *do* with your creative material within the givens is what we are discussing here.

My colleague Chuck Waterman reminds me that—since my system involves keeping all options open as long as possible—I shouldn't *entirely* rule out making an outline. Says Chuck:

> Some kinds of creative writing are indeed organized carefully before the author begins the actual writing task. Among these are mystery and detective stories, where the writer conceives the solution and works backward toward the problem A good example of this is almost any Perry Mason mystery; Erle Stanley Gardner, a lawyer before he became a writer, loved to build an entire plot around a keypoint of law.
>
> The outline we are speaking of here is more of a thread of the story that will have to be pursued if all the plotlines are to meet in the big surprise finale.

Even here, of course, the writer does not use a Roman numeral, cap A, etc. In this format, the writer may draw something that looks more like a computer diagram or a calendar, or a map, than it does like an outline.

Chuck's points are well taken, even though this chapter is primarily concerned with report writing, not "creative writing." Also, as you will find, I haven't ruled out making an outline; I have simply replaced the "conventional" outline method, which usually doesn't work, with an "easy way" that always does.

What's the problem?

The first step in writing is to identify your subject. You must know exactly what you want to accomplish, or the project will never get off the ground. In considering this, focus your approach on the basic truth that most reports are concerned, one way or another, with stating a problem and offering a possible solution or solutions.

But reports are often written without full knowledge of the facts. Indeed, many of them should never see the light of day. My first advice to anyone assigned the project of turning out a report is: "Get out of it if possible!" That comment is not entirely facetious. What I mean is that you should start by doing some basic research—find out what is already in print, and what information on the subject is readily available.

The wheel is being re-invented almost every day. At NASA they still talk about a large aerospace company, back in the days of Project Mercury, which spent two million dollars and a year of research on a project. When at last the report was published, THEN somebody discovered a competitor had performed almost identical research, come up with the same results, and published a report that could have been purchased for $14.95! This story sounds too true to be apocryphal.

So, before you begin to think about writing *anything*, hie yourself to the library, enlist the aid of a technical librarian, and find out who has written what. Even if this research doesn't save you from having to write your own report, knowing what is already in print will enable you to do your job a whole lot better.

Again, Chuck Waterman has some words of wisdom on the subject:

Don't rely on the library alone. Consult *all* available documents in your own office: worksheets, lab reports, data printouts, program objective statements, headshed memos, project notebooks, workbooks, test results, and anything else that seems appropriate.

Beyond that, interview (other) experts and perhaps even visit a lab or test station to get hard data on the spot. You may have to look at miles of 16 mm movie film or reams of accordian-fold computer printouts to find the miserable two or three nuggets for a 16-page report.

As your store of background information and hard supporting data grows, you'll discover that what you already know will help disclose what else you'll *need* to know. All the time, you should be taking notes. Use the card system you learned in high school or college composition courses. In case you've grown rusty on this, here are a few reminders:

Bibliography cards

Use standard 3 x 5 cards. Make a separate card for each reference you check. Put on each card, in the order indicated, the items listed below:

- *Author's name,* last name first. If the book has more than one author, list the rest of the names, first names first, in order that they appear on the title page of the book.
- *Title of publication,* underscored. (If you're listing an article from a magazine or periodical, put the title of the article itself in quotation marks. Then give the name of the magazine and underscore it.)
- *The edition* (1st, 2d, etc.)
- *Name of publisher*
- *Place of publication*
- *Date of publication* (if no date is given, write n.d.)

In the lower left corner of the card, place the library call number or file number. That way, you'll have it handy and won't have to look it up again if you need to track down the reference later.

In the upper right corner of the card, write your own identifying number, starting with "1" on the first card and continuing with consecutive numbers on succeeding cards. You will refer to these numbers to identify the source of your *note cards.* You don't need to be concerned about alphabetizing at this point. You'll do that later, when you prepare the actual bibliography or list of references for your report or paper.

Thomas, Lewis ①
The Medusa and the Snail
New York: The Viking Press,
1979

Excellent essays,
espec. one on
punctuation

Bibliography card

Notes on Punctuation ①
Lewis Thomas makes cogent observa-
tions about the four stops—comma,
semicolon, colon, and period.
He makes a special point about
the values of the semicolon.
Also good advice on quotation
MARKS.

pp. 125-129

Note card

Note cards

After you survey a reference work and decide it will be useful, take careful notes in a way that permits you to identify what idea came from what source. Many experts recommend 3 x 5 cards for this; certainly that size is convenient, but 4 x 6 or 5 x 8 may be better. Do you frequently have to carry over material from one card to another? Then you'll find the larger cards much easier to handle.

You might want to use different colors for the various types of material—for example, yellow for bibliography cards, white for the related note cards, and blue for your original material.

Most standard references on report writing suggest that you write notes in your own words, rather than quoting the author exactly. When you do quote a writer's own words, *enclose them in quotation marks. Quotations must be exact, even to vagaries in grammar, spelling, or punctuation.* Use the expression *sic* (Latin for *thus*) to indicate mistakes or special usages for which the original writer is responsible.

In quoted material, indicate omitted words by ellipses (. . .).

If you find it necessary to add any of your own words in a quoted passage, enclose them in brackets. ([ ]).

There are certain cases when direct quotations are necessary and helpful. For example, when—

- The point is important.
- The statement is to be refuted.
- The author's statement is ambiguous.
- The citation may be questioned.
- The point is stated so well that the style will strengthen your own report or paper.

Often you will make a number of note cards from the same reference. Make sure to cross-index each note card with the appropriate bibliography card, using a number system that corresponds with that of the bibliography cards.

Take down more notes and quotations than you expect to use. Err on the side of too much rather than too little. This practice will save you time and trouble when you actually get down to writing.

The easy way to outline

I'm putting what follows in boldface, to emphasize how important this material is. What you are about to read is the most practical system for making an outline that really works that I have gleaned during a lifetime of writing. Here is the system, which emphasizes my profound belief: KEEP ALL OPTIONS OPEN AS LONG AS POSSIBLE.

● **Get a batch of 5 x 8 notecards.(All right, get 3 x 5 or 4 x 6 if you feel you must, but 5 x 8 cards are much better, for reasons we'll presently discuss.)**

● *Brainstorm.* **Throw your imagination into high gear, and start putting down ideas about your project. If you can persuade fellow workers or colleagues who are familiar with your project to help you—and this is what the term "brainstorming" really means, the way it is done in advertising agencies—by all means do so. Creativity is compounded; one idea sparks another. (Remember, no one is allowed to criticize anyone else's idea, no matter how far out it may seem at the time.)**

If you end up like the little red hen, with no help, apply the brainstorming process on yourself. Turn your subconscious mind loose. You don't have to know or care where a particular idea is going to fit. All you need do is write it down. Maybe it will eventually land in the first section, or the middle, or the last. You couldn't (or needn't care less at this point. (NOTE: Apply the process at your most creative time of day—for most of us that would be fairly early in the morning, but not if you are a night person.)

● **Put each idea down on a *separate* card. (Just a few words will be sufficient—write only enough to remind you of the idea later.)**

● **As soon as you complete a card, put it aside. Use a fresh card for the next idea. The beauty of this approach is that it frees you from the whole routine of having to figure out in advance what is important. You aren't concerned with what is going to be subordinated to what. It is really a joyful experience to be so free and easy, and to know that you are not locking yourself in.**

● Work on a different project for the rest of the day. (This is important—it relaxes your mind so that when you tackle the job again, you'll be fresh and ready for it.)

● Take the cards home with you; read through them just before you go to sleep. That way, your subconscious mind will do much of the hard work for you. Try it. It works.

● Next morning, spread out the cards where you can see them. As you try arranging the cards in various sequences, you can begin shaping them up into an increasingly logical order. As you proceed, you may move cards forward or back in the sequence as ideas begin to gel. Put closely related cards in the same row or stack.

● As you study the cards, sometimes a phrase, a sentence, or even a whole paragraph may come to mind on how to develop a particular point. Stop right there—*write the thought down directly on the card* before those inspired words escape forever. (That's why I like the 5 x 8 cards; they give more room to write down thoughts. Often by the time I've finished arranging the cards in sequence, I've got a big headstart on the report.)

● When you finally get the cards into an order you like, use them to make a formal outline. You're safe in doing this, because your options are still open. The outline isn't etched on stone, so if things don't work out quite right, you can always shuffle the deck and try again. (Incidentally, when I was writing speeches at NASA, I *never* threw any of those cards away. Sometimes by a bit of thoughtful shuffling, I could come up with several different speeches from the same set of cards!)

● At this point, use the cards as building blocks. Build on each card, by expanding an idea to a sentence, a sentence to a paragraph. The stronger you can make each card, the easier your actual writing will be when the time comes. My experience has been that sometimes the report gets more than half finished while it's still on cards. Can't beat that.

That's it—the whole secret. It works so well it's almost scary. By comparison, if you had used a conventional approach, as soon as you wrote your ideas in even the most random of orders on a single sheet of paper, they would have begun to set harder than concrete and a whole lot faster. That seems to be the way human thought processes work: put something down on a page, and even though the order turns out (as random orders usually do) to be illogical or unworkable, your mind (subconscious?) works to justify (rationalize) its illogic. You often find the jumble impossible to change. You'll hate the helpless feeling of being stuck with an arrangement you know in your heart is wrong.

The conventional response at this point is the old scissors-and-staple-ploy—cut up sentences and paragraphs and staple them into a new order, until the project looks like a feather duster that has seen better days. You know what a mess that is.

So, one more time: *Use the card system. Keep all options open as long as you possibly can.*

Visualize the total report

Once you have a working outline, fit it into the standard format your organization uses. A good way to start is to study a *good* existing report. (For heaven's sake, don't choose a poor example as your standard.)

Make a simple "dummy" of the project, and your task will be much easier. The usual report is divided into three major sections, the *Introduction,* the *Body* (or *Discussion*), and the *Conclusion.* In addition, there will be "front matter" consisting usually of a *letter of transmittal,* a *summary* or *abstract, table of contents,* and sometimes a *list of figures and tables.* If you have extremely complex or technical material that might slow your pace in the body of the report, consider putting it separately, in an *appendix.* Many readers will ignore such material, but specialists will dote on it.

Here is another way to cut a big job down to size. I'll tell you what I do; then you may want to try your own variations. The objective, whatever device you use, is to break that overwhelming multi-page report into bitesized pieces. The difference this makes in psychological attitude is astounding: small pieces, no matter how many, seem far easier to deal with.

I use file folders with internal pockets—one on each side—that hold standard sheets of paper. I label one folder for each section of the job and put my notecards into the appropriate folders, using the lefthand pockets. As the report grows, the sheets of typed material go into the righthand pockets.

When the first draft is completely typed, I check against the cards to make sure I haven't missed anything; then I file them. The first typing now moves to the left; the new revised draft will go to the right. Watching the folders fill is encouraging, helping you to maintain a full head of steam.

Footnotes, credits and references

Footnotes can be helpful for both writer and reader. I originally intended to use footnotes in this book, but as an amateur who enjoys setting my own type, I was not up to the technicalities of fitting the footnotes evenly at the bottom margins of the pages. I chickened out and listed my references in parentheses instead—not scholarly looking, perhaps, but much easier to set in type.

The reports *you* turn out will probably be done on a typewriter. In that case, footnotes are easy, and I suggest you use them. One good thing about this time-honored device, is that you can keep your narrative going full tilt without slowing the pace with meticulous details. Using footnotes, the extra information is there for anyone who wants it.

Your "everyday" readers are interested primarily in the narrative; they can read straight through and skip the footnotes. If you have specialist readers concerned with minute details, the situation remains well under control. Writer and readers share the best of all possible worlds.

But footnotes should be used properly, and *located* properly. My pet peeve is the chintzy method—used by many publishers—of putting all footnotes, bunched together, at the end of a chapter or clear at the back of the book. This leaves the reader with several choices, all miserable. One choice involves reading through the chapter and then going back and reading the footnotes. This is frustrating because the reader forgets what the footnotes are referring to. The alternative is just as bad—flip-flopping back and forth between the text and the footnotes—an extremely time-consuming and frustrating operation.

I've been talking here about *explanatory* footnotes. *Documentation* is different. It's okay to list authors, references, and the like, at the end, if this method makes life easier for the production staff.

For more guidance on footnotes and scholarly citations, you shouldn't have any trouble finding a suitable stylebook—quite likely, your organization has one, or more. If not, a good (and inexpensive) choice is Kate L. Turabian's *A Manual for Writers of Term Papers, Theses and Dissertations.* (Chicago: University of Chicago Press, 1973.)

Finally, when the report has been put together, alphabetize your bibliography cards and use them as the basis of your *Bibliography* or *List of References* section. This is where you list all your sources, whether you have actually quoted directly from them or not. However, one word of warning: don't frustrate readers by listing "classified" (top secret, secret, confidential, etc.) sources or other items difficult or impossible to obtain. If you *must* mention such documents, make sure to indicate their status, so as not to send anyone on a goose chase.

Using copyright material

Incidentally, if you publish a report containing quotations from copyrighted sources, give credit where credit is due. Clearly identify all such material and attribute it properly. If you plan to quote more than a few words of copyrighted material from any one source, obtain formal permission from the copyright owner to use it. Read the section on *Copyright* in the handbook section of this book; for more detailed information, a good source is *Law and the Writer,* edited by Kirk Polking and Leonard S. Meranus. (Cincinnati, Ohio: Writer's Digest Books, 1978.)

Summing up

I realize we've covered considerable territory in this chapter, but I urge you to master it. Follow the instructions faithfully and you'll turn out reports better and faster than ever before.

A final reminder: for maximum efficiency, always separate the *writing* and *editing* aspects of your work. This is important even for short pieces; it is imperative for long ones. Don't try to edit as you write—get those words down on paper as fast as you can, and edit them later. For more suggestions on increasing efficiency, see Chapter 15.

Axiom Six:

WRITE —

REWRITE —

REWRITE

Writing is like walking blindfold: instinct will carry you far, but not always where you want to go. Before long, the instinct-guided writer, like the blinded walker, bumps into things. Like the hard question of when to write. Everyone knows that Hemingway liked to write in the morning, Mark Twain when he was lying down, H. L. Mencken when he sniffed a deadline, and Norman Mailer whenever he gets punched in the mouth . . .

—*Colman McCarthy,* Inner Companions

15: How to Write like a Professional

Establishing good writing habits

One of the most well-organized and self-disciplined writers I've ever known is Virgil Carrington "Pat" Jones. I hope you've had the pleasure of reading some of his work. He's a recognized authority on everything from the War Between the States to the real story of the Hatfields and the McCoys. His *Gray Ghosts and Rebel Raiders* served as the inspiration for the popular "Gray Ghost" television series of a few years back.

It was my privilege to share an office at NASA Headquarters with Pat Jones for several years. He was one of several extremely talented writers who worked in my shop. I sometimes wondered why it wasn't the other way around. Anyway, when I first met Pat, he was working on a book, even though he was also employed full-time as a NASA ghostwriter. For Pat, that was par for the course.

How did he do it? By getting out of bed at 2:30 every morning and working straight through until breakfast. Pat has been following this demanding routine every morning, seven days a week, for many, many years. (He's still doing it.) And that was only the beginning. After putting in three or four hours of writing and research, Pat would eat breakfast, drive about forty miles into Washington through the rush hour traffic, and be at his desk next to mine promptly at 8:15 — or usually earlier. There he would sit, straight as a ramrod, all day long, turning out more and better copy than many other writers half his age. That is real self-discipline!

Pat Jones' advice

As an aspiring middle-aged writer, I often asked Pat for advice. He gave it kindly and freely. I haven't always had the gumption to take it, but it's a pleasure to pass some of his wisdom on to you. Here are some of the important things he told me:

Try to write at the same time every day. Set up a regular routine and stick to it. Make it a habit. You have to learn what time of day is best for you — Pat is a morning person; other writers I know don't begin to function until the sun goes down — then work at your writing at that time, systematically, every day.

Don't stop — or even slow down — once you "get up to speed." Work at least three or four hours, until you feel yourself growing genuinely tired. Pat says it's okay to take a few minutes for a break every hour or so, allowing that the best of us may need to go to the bathroom once in a while. Also, he says, walking around taking a few deep breaths will help relax those muscles at the back of the neck. They seem to get even more tired than your posterior does when you've been sitting in front of your typewriter for a long spell.

Don't let anything interrupt you. This is one of several reasons Pat likes those early morning hours — no telephone calls or other annoying intrusions on concentration.

Make your surroundings conducive to good work. After I moved to Fairfax, Virginia, I seized the opportunity to visit Pat in his home, which is situated in a beautiful wooded area. His land was once a battlefield; it even has a historical marker at one corner of his front yard. Pat, who is as handy with tools as he is with a typewriter, built his own office. It covers most of the top floor of his house. Bookshelves line every wall; every book is catalogued. (Pat can even tell you the date he finished reading each book.) His many file cabinets are all clearly labeled. Within arm's reach of his desk is an ingenious four-sided revolving bookshelf that holds all the references he must check most frequently during a particular project.

At each end of his office are huge windows. Just outside is a balcony where he sometimes sets up his typewriter when the weather is right. From his desk he can see woods and what we Virginians call a "run."

I envy all Pat's arrangements except the view. For someone with my lack of self-discipline, it would be murder. My own office doesn't even have a window. I have long since discovered that I would rather admire scenery than sit at my typewriter and tackle a difficult writing task. My self-discipline improves only when I face austere surroundings and an inescapable deadline.

Don't try to write when you are "starving to death," having a nicotine fit, or are wornout and exhausted. It's hard enough to work when you're fresh and have everything going for you. Don't make things any harder for yourself than you have to. If you aren't careful, you could actually build a conditioned reflex *against* writing. (I don't smoke, so I don't have *that* problem at first hand.) One of my fellow ghosts at NASA was constantly trying to give up cigarettes. Like Mark Twain, he had "done it a thousand times." When he didn't have any writing pressures on him, he could hold out bravely. He would go on for hours or days without a single drag from the noxious weed.

But let a deadline assignment come up, and he couldn't cajole a word out of his typewriter unless he had a cigarette dangling from his lips. Smoking was, to him, such an ingrained habit that it had become a conditioned response. It was, and still is, an inescapable part of his whole creative process.

Production rates for writers

How many pages of manuscript should a disciplined writer be able to turn out in a day's work?

There aren't any standard answers. Writing speeds, even among professional writers, seem to vary all over the lot.

Still, after observing dozens of writers (some of them professionals, and a helluva lot more who were not), I'll stick my neck out. In my opinion, a good average would probably be *about five to ten double-spaced, typewritten pages a day.*

If you manage that kind of production, you can be confident that the boss has no right to complain. But let's elaborate on this subject a bit. Bear in mind that, even with *professional* writers, production rates can and do vary considerably from day to day. What is more important to a disciplined pro is that those five or ten pages represent his or her best efforts.

Let me tell you about another of the really fine professional writers I have known — my former boss and longtime mentor, James R. Aswell. I worked with Jim for almost a decade, and never ceased to marvel at his dedication to excellence. Many times I have watched him put his daily five or ten pages of copy through the equivalent of four — or even five — separate and complete drafts. Each would be slightly different from, and undeniably better than, the one that went before. Katie Egland, the patient and long suffering secretary who typed our manuscripts, would put on her most resigned look. Then she'd bravely type another draft from Jim's henscratch revisions. She knew, and we all knew, full well that she would be typing at least three or four more versions before the day was out.

I once overheard Jim's boss say, "That damned Aswell — everything he writes is for the Pulitzer Prize." Well, the boss may have thought he was putting Jim down with that remark. The scorn for Jim's dogged and continuing search for writing perfection was not the least bit subtle. But to me — and, I feel quite sure, to Jim himself, if he had known about it — the remark wasn't a putdown at all. It was the highest possible compliment. For, in all the years I've known him, and that has been almost a quarter of a century, one fact stands out: James R. Aswell is constitutionally incapable of writing *anything* without giving it his best shot.

Another of my ghostwriting colleagues at NASA was Jack Doherty, a former newspaperman who had covered the White House beat for the *New York Daily News.* Like many other ex-newspapermen, Jack found it difficult to get up a head of steam until a deadline had him cornered. Once in that position, with no possible escape, Jack could write like an angel. He could turn out four or five double-spaced pages of really "singing" copy in less than an hour. I suspect that not too many writers in this world can manage that much production. An average of about two pages an hour, or roughly 500 words, probably is closer to the norm.

All I can say is, don't let any of this scare you. You —my readers — are almost undoubtedly not professional writers. Granted. Still, you are writing on a subject you know about — you're the expert. Use the tricks I've shown you, and you can produce as much as a pro, day in and day out. Realistically, neither you nor I will expect you to turn out prizewinning prose. But I *do* expect, and I hope you'll agree, that you'll produce five to ten pages of clear, *useful writing* every day that your job requires it. You *can* do it — and I hope you will.

AXIOM SIX. Rewrite — rewrite — rewrite!

The mechanics of writing production

Most writers who do not type their own manuscripts have no idea of how long it takes simply to perform the *mechanical* details of getting a manuscript out: typing, collating, stapling, distributing, and so on. Even the most experienced executives are likely to have a vague notion that a person who holds a typing job in a business office or a government agency should be able to type at least 40 to 50 words a minute — minimum. Furthermore, they have probably read somewhere that really proficient typists can go much faster than that — 60, 70, perhaps even 80 words a minute.

Well, they're right in theory, but wrong in practice. What they don't know is that nothing in this world is ever that simple. You can't just count up the total number of words in a manuscript, divide by 80 words a minute (or 70, or 60, or whatever) and come up with a time estimate.

For one thing, this simplistic approach doesn't begin to allow for all the other necessary but time-consuming details that executives are not accustomed to thinking about. The typist has to line up an original (bond paper) copy with about umpteen different colored carbon copies. Then, if the typing is done on a regular office typewriter, the typist encounters problems that would curdle the blood. Every single time one wrong character is struck, the procedure is to insert a shield behind the carbons, one at a time, and erase each sheet separately. Murder!

If you are fortunate enough to work in a shop that has automatic word processing equipment, the typist can correct mistakes simply by backspacing and striking the key for the correct character. This saves much time — but not so much as you might think. What you may not have realized is that the finished rough draft, even though it has been corrected, is not the final product. Each page must be run through again. Even at 175 words or more a minute (which many of the late model machines can easily do) this takes an extra couple of minutes for *each page*. Also, we still have not allowed for the inevitable interruptions that most typists face constantly — answering the telephone, hunting things up in the files, getting coffee for you, the boss, and visiting dignitaries.

Ask the most competent typist you know how many words a day are turned out, in finished form, on an average day, and the answer will probably surprise you.

Would you believe that the year-round average of production in American offices is *about three lines of typing per minute?* I didn't make this figure up. It comes straight from a formal study conducted a year or so ago by a magazine called *The Secretary.* Thus, the average letter or report will be typed at a rate of approximately *five pages an hour* — certainly no faster.

One thing you need to know — and you probably don't — is how many words you usually get on a typewritten page. I suggest that you try a few experiments. Figure out how many words per page, on the average, you put in your own writing. It's an awfully handy figure to know.

I type my own final drafts. You probably don't. When I finish typing, the work is ready to go. But if you are going to be turning your copy over to a secretary or a word processing center, you must allow for a built-in time lag of between two and three hours before your product can go out. You cannot relax and assume you've met your deadline when you have turned your draft over to the typist. Remember: *allow time for all the required mechanical steps — these may include not only the typing, but perhaps also such other time-consuming processes as duplicating, sorting, collating, stapling, and distributing.* I wish I had a dollar (or a nickel, for that matter) for every time that a writer has completed the job itself on time, but has missed a deadline because of not having allowed for the built-in delay factors. *If you're wise, you'll put a fudge factor in your planning.*

AXIOM SEVEN. Allow in your planning for production delays.

Deadlines and supervisors

Many so-called "management experts" — who, as a concomitant fringe benefit of their position can set deadlines for working writers — do not have the faintest idea how long a writing job should take. Unfortunately, it is very difficult to explain to them the facts of life. They often have the obtuse mentality that is inevitably prevalent among those who can draw their pay without having to write themselves. (If you detect a note of bitterness, you're right!) Nothing can be so exasperating as having to explain, with great care, what some of the problems are, only to hear the response, "That's all very well, but have the manuscript on my desk by close of business today." Those rotten (expletives deleted) obviously do not hear a word of what you say.

Chances are, you'll run into another problem — not quite so bad, but still plenty bad enough. Your supervisor will come charging in and say, "I want you to do a report on (fill in an appropriate subject). How long is it going to take?"

How does anyone answer a question like that? I've never found out. Until you've done some research, you can't possibly have any idea what the job requires. You won't know whether you'll have to look up all sorts of obscure data. You also won't know whether you will be lucky enough to find some quick resources, so that difficult questions are already sorted out in advance.

It's a good bet that you will have to send out of town for certain items. There are always imponderables — problems that cannot possibly be predicted.

Well, one thing you can do with these obtuse characters is to quote an authority. Here's one that might carry a certain amount of weight: *Writing Guide for Naval Officers,* published by the U.S. Government Printing Office. Because the book has been out of print for some years, I'll do you a favor and quote some of the appropriate passages here:

> Estimating writing time is a difficult process. Some reporters and fiction writers can turn out a million words a year, the equivalent of a 20-page report every day. But the author of one hundred western stories a year will find his production slowed down if he undertakes a new form of writing. He'll have to do research. He'll have to think out new lines of action, characters, and dialogue. Similarly, a newspaper reporter can write rapidly about what he observes; he can report on what people say and do. But assign him the task of reporting in depth or analyzing the reasons and the trends behind events and he too will sweat over his words.

Let me pause for an "aside" here, before continuing the quotation. In the late 1950s, Jim Aswell and I worked for a couple of years with a gifted writer named Norvell Page. (Norvell was an ex-writer of pulp-paper thrillers. For those of you too young to remember, pulp-paper magazines were what old galoots like me used to read before World War II — the predecessors of today's comic books.)

For most of a decade, Norvell Page had turned out, single-handed, an entire magazine, called *The Spider*. (Don't confuse this with today's comic book *Spiderman*.) Each month, Page would have to write a lead novelette of at least 80 printed pages. Then he would write a half dozen or so short stories, not connected with his main novelette in any way. *The Spider* magazine would be roughly 200 printed pages per month, all written by *one man,* month after month, year after year.

That's an incredible performance. It would give the willies to most of the professional writers I know. That kind of pressure might be okay once in a while, but not when sustained over months and years.

Just for comparison, and this is a comparison *to,* not a comparison with: The complete works of Shakespeare total slightly more than one million words. The complete King James translation of the Holy Bible also adds up to something more than one million words. Norvell Page annually turned out more than a half-million words of not-quite-so-deathless prose for many, many years.

In all the history of writing, only a handful of writers have done that. In modern times, Dr. Isaac Asimov probably takes the cake. By the time this book gets to press, Asimov will have turned out more than 200 books, and he's still going strong. Erle Stanley Gardner, of *Perry Mason* fame, broke a few records; so did the French writer of detective stories, Georges Simenon. Add to the list Zane Grey, Edgar Rice Burroughs, Kenneth Robeson (creator of *Doc Savage;* Robeson's real name was Lester Dent). Add Max Brand, whose real name I can't remember, and a few others, and that just about does it. In earlier times, add Charles Dickens (who was accused by his contemporaries of writing potboilers), Victor Hugo, Alexander Dumas, and a few more. Yes, Norvell Page was one of a rather select group when it comes to production. He had things down to a formula—a formula that worked great for grinding out pulp detective stories and science fiction.

But now the scene changes. When Jim and I worked for Norvell Page, he was in charge of producing the Atomic Energy Commission's Semiannual Report to Congress. And believe me, Norvell didn't crank out that complicated opus in a couple of weeks. The task took months of effort on his part, and he had the incredible talents of Jim Aswell and me to back him up.

The moral of this true-life fable is that you may hear wondrous recitals about the enormous productivity and speed of a given writer in a given situation. Those stories may well be true. But — keep in mind the chastening truth that the dazzling speed will inevitably slow to a crawl any time the writer is forced to tackle assignments that fall outside the familiar territory.

Okay, it's time to return to the Navy treatise. Again I quote:

> A captain with considerable experience advised students at the Naval War College concerning their term papers. He recommended that they allocate at least two hours a day over a two-month period to prepare papers running from 8,000 to 12,000 words. [He was, of course, addressing students, not professional writers.]
>
> The famous novelist and short-story writer, W. Somerset Maugham, once remarked that in his experience a professional writer can write at most about three hours a day. He knew of some authors that wrote only one hour a day, and he admitted that others might sometimes go on for ten, twelve, and even sixteen hours at a stretch. But, he added, such authors usually balanced out productive periods with weeks in which they wrote little or nothing. The average administrator cannot expect to concentrate on a writing task for more than three hours a day, and often these hours must be spread out because of the other demands of the job.
>
> For most administrators whose writing is assigned as a secondary task, you may very well be spending about one-third of your time in actual writing.

Department of anticlimax

For fourteen chapters I've regaled you with the best advice on useful writing that I know how to give. Of the wondrous things I've told you, what's good is probably not original, and what's original may or may not be good. (Don't be taken in by my false modesty. That statement itself is a mild paraphrase of a famous putdown of a would-be author. The great lexicographer Samuel Johnson, one of the top putdown artists of all time, is the source of this particular "borrowing.")

Very little that is new has been written on the subject of writing — any kind of writing — since the time of Aristotle. But I do hope I've hung a few new ornaments on the ancient Christmas tree. I sincerely hope, also, that you have at least been reminded of some important things you may once have known but have probably forgotten. And I hope even more that you may have gained a new perspective — a way of looking at things so that you will be *motivated*. Get that missionary spirit— strive to improve all the copy you must write or edit.

Go forth and preach the gospel. Whatever you can do will be a help to your customers or clients or the taxpayers, as the case may be — and that's you and me. In your spare time, please browse through the handbook section that follows. (There's an explanation of what this is all about on page 134.

As a writer, I'm aware that I've made heavy demands on your time and trouble. If you've stuck with me this far, thanks for your courage.

And now, I pray you, keep the faith. (And read the handbook.)

Axiom Seven:

ALLOW IN YOUR
PLANNING FOR
PRODUCTION
DELAYS

PART TWO

HANDBOOK SECTION

HOW TO USE THE HANDBOOK

This handbook section does not pretend to be complete. It simply explains, in plain language, a few terms, techniques, and usages that working writers need to know. Use it to augment the information contained in Part One.

For convenience, the handbook is arranged in alphabetical order. There are just two exceptions:

Under the heading **grammar — a few elementary principles,** you will find, *not* in alphabetical order, the following items: **nouns, pronouns, number, case, direct objects, indirect objects, verbs, person and number of verbs, transitive and intransitive verbs, adjectives, conjunctions,** and **prepositions.** Some of this grouping duplicates other material found elsewhere. I have put them all in one unit here because of the inter-relationships of the items being discussed.

Similarly, under the heading **sentence — the parts of,** you will find discussions of **subject, predicate, direct object,** and **indirect object.** Again there is a small amount of duplication. Again the duplication is intentional. This is in keeping with my belief that we should try to make individual discussions stand on their own feet — within reasonable limits!

Readers have a right to ask why I did not also explain other grammatical terms such as *clauses, phrases, complements,* and so on. Perhaps I should have. But we have only so much space, and I have tried to limit my discussions to the items that will be of the most immediate and practical value to most readers. There are dozens of excellent references easily available on all these subjects. Check the bibliography for recommendations.

I would suggest that you read straight through this handbook section. It covers much important material not touched on in Part One.

Please be sure to read the entry under **he/she dilemma (sexism in language).** This can be found on pages 159-160. There you will find some guidelines on a very important subject that has not been covered before in any writing handbook of which I am aware.

● ability/capacity

Ability is the power to do something; *capacity* is the power to receive something. You can acquire ability, but you must be born with capacity. Ability can be improved by practice; capacity isn't helped by all the hard work in the world. You can keep the difference straight by picturing the ability of a skilled athlete, on the one hand, versus the capacity of a carton or receptacle, on the other.

●abbreviations and acronyms

Most administrative writing is riddled with abbreviations and acronyms. An abbreviation, as you know, is a shortened or contracted word or phrase, used to represent the whole. An acronym is a word made up by combining the first one or two letters from each of a group of words.

To communicate clearly, make sure not to use abbreviations or acronyms without explaining them *unless you are absolutely sure that everyone in your audience will be familiar with them*. Remember that many readers will not have the slightest idea what these shorthand expressions mean.

Play it safe. If there is any doubt in your mind that even a few readers will be unfamiliar with your terms, you should *spell out* each abbreviation or acronym the first time you use it. Then put the acronym or abbreviation in parentheses. From then on, you can safely use the shortened version. However, if you explain the meaning early in a piece of writing, but do not use the short form again for many pages, don't expect your reader to remember. Spell it out again!

The best and funniest explanation of acronyms I have ever encountered can be found in a witty and perceptive spoof of bureaucracy called *The Kidner Report*. I quote:

> . . . Acronymizing is the art of making words by combining the first one or two letters in a group of words. The function is to simplify communications by reducing oft-repeated, complex titles and phrases to a set of initials. However, the acronym must spell something pronounceable; otherwise an abbreviation results, and this is too pedestrian.
>
> The technique is to choose a word to be spelled, then construct the title to yield it. In doing so, remember that the word should be easy to pronounce, and it shouldn't spell anything dirty in any language.
>
> Dirty words sneak up even when merely writing titles and phrases without ever intending to make acronyms out of them. Since I write a lot of government papers, I always keep this rule before me: *Be Absolutely Sure That Acronyms Reflect Decency*. Indeed, an experienced acronymist converts to an acronym almost unconsciously any time he sees two or more words that are capitalized or appear to have been assembled more for their first letters than their meaning.

— *The Kidner Report,* pp. 45-46

● active voice (see voice, active and passive — use of)

● accusative

This term is really taken from Latin grammar, but some teachers of English still use it to indicate the *objective case* — the *direct object* of a verb. For example, "John loves *Mary.*"

● adjective

A part of speech that modifies or changes the meaning of a *noun* or *pronoun.*

● adverb

A word that modifies or changes the meaning of a *verb,* an *adjective,* or another *adverb.* Many adverbs — but not all of them — end in the suffix *-ly.* Examples: *quickly, slowly, steadily, belatedly.*

● ad nauseam

Should a writer use foreign-sounding words such as this? *Sometimes.* The expression, of course, is Latin, but it's also acceptable English. It means *to a sickening degree,* but expresses the idea more succinctly. It may not be one of your everyday words, but it can be useful on occasion. Indeed, sometimes it's the *mot juste.* (Which, incidentally, is another case in point — an expression that is extremely useful in certain contexts.)

● almanac

Every writer should have one of these useful one-volume compendiums. (This is another Latin word that's also useful English. A compendium is a brief summary. The plural is as I've used it, not *compendia.)* A good almanac will give you information that's hard or impossible to find anywhere else — items such as the longest rivers, the highest mountains, the biggest cities. Or even what Joe DiMaggio's batting average was when he played with the San Francisco Seals, or what horse won the Kentucky Derby in 1936.

A good almanac is a trivia lover's delight. One of my Army friends used to memorize entire sections of the World Almanac. Then he'd go to the nearest bar, make outlandish bets, and win. He raked in a lot of money, but he was also punched in the nose with some regularity.

There are so many excellent almanacs on the market that I won't single one out — go to your nearest bookstore and browse.

● alphabetical order

Never underestimate the value of alphabetical order in lining up items so that they will be easy to find and easy to understand. Since the advent of "Sesame Street," children learn the alphabet even before they start to school. They are comfortable, because they can understand what letter comes before or after some other letter, even if they can't comprehend more complex systems of order. So — don't sell alphabetical listings short. They can be very useful in achieving clear communication.

● ambiguity — how to avoid

Ambiguity is one of the greatest hazards a writer encounters when striving for precision and clarity. If readers can possibly misinterpret, they undoubtedly will. (See *Murphy's Law.)*The fact is, many times the reader will misinterpret even if the writer has taken special care to remove any possibility of ambiguity. Sad, but true.

Here are some common causes of ambiguity. Notice that each of the following examples can be interpreted in several different ways.

FAULTY PRONOUN REFERENCE. *John told Jim that he was fired.* Is the "he" John or Jim? The reader can't tell. Rewrite the sentence something like this: *John told Jim, "You're fired!"* Or, *John had been fired, and told Jim about it.*

MISPLACED MODIFIERS. Place your modifiers carefully, as close as possible to the words they are intended to modify. Sometimes the results of a misplaced modifier are laughable but harmless. Sometimes they can be downright misleading. One of my favorites is a headline from a news story that appeared in the *Washington Post*. It went like this: *POLICEMAN SHOOTS THIEF WITH KNIFE*

DANGLING MODIFIERS. These are verbal clusters that either (a) have nothing to modify; or (b) give the appearance of modifying a word other than the one intended. Usually they are introductory phrases, such as:

DANGLING: *Walking down the street, a strange sight came into my view.*

CORRECTED: *As I was walking down the street, a strange sight came into my view.* (This "correction" is grammatically correct, but stylistically poor, because of an *unnecessary shift.* How about " . . *I saw a strange sight"?*)

OTHER COMMON CAUSES OF AMBIGUITY. There are, of course, many other possible causes of multiple meanings. One of the most common stems from using a word that can be defined in several different ways in a context that makes for confusion or absurdity. For example, *After waiting for a brief period, he changed the comma to a semicolon.*

Another error involves failing to make clear the "field of operation" of a word or phrase. For example, analyze the adverb *more* in this sentence: *The child needs to be given more nourishing food.* (Greater quantities of food? Or food with improved nutritional qualities?) Here's another example, this time involving a negative: *This report was not submitted because of information received.*

Sometimes you can get rid of an ambiguity by using punctuation, but unless you go to the trouble of correcting the sentence itself, this would-be remedy is often sloppy and ineffective. The late lamented H. W. Fowler once wrote: "It may almost be said that what reads wrongly if the stops are removed is radically bad; stops are not to alter meaning but merely to show it up."

Ambiguity can creep up on us in many guises. Here's a beautiful example of a type that hasn't been illustrated so far. I think I first ran across this gem in *Reader's Digest.*

(Sign posted in a cafeteria:)
SHOES ARE REQUIRED TO EAT IN THIS CAFETERIA.
Underneath the print on the sign, some wag had pencilled:
SOCKS CAN EAT WHEREVER THEY WANT TO.

● alumnus

Like other Latin words, this one gives most of us Americans trouble. Here's everything you need to know in one easy lesson:

Masculine singular: *alumnus,* pronounced uh-LUM-nus
Masculine plural: *alumni,* pronounced uh-LUM-NYE
Feminine singular: *alumna,* pronounced uh-LUM-nuh
Feminine plural: *alumnae,* pronounced uh-LUM-nee.

__The Romans were a bunch of male chauvinist pigs (like some others we won't mention), so when you refer to a mixed group of men and women, you are automatically locked in to using the word used for the masculine plural: *alumni.*

● amount/number

Amount is used to refer to things thought of in bulk (sometimes called *mass nouns*). *Number* is used to refer to things that you can count as individual items. Thus, you would say "The *amount* of material wasted last week was a scandal." But you would say, "The number of employees late for work yesterday was higher than at any other time in recent history."

● analogy

An *analogy* is a *comparison* between two objects or concepts. Use this device to show your reader as clearly as you can the ways in which the items you are comparing are similar. For example, you might say *Rain is to snow as water is to ice.*

Analogies are great for defining terms, explaining processes, or elucidating abstract ideas.

● and/or

Try to avoid using *and/or* whenever you possibly can. It is a clumsy and awkward way of expressing the idea that either (a) both circumstances are possible, or (b) only one of two circumstances is possible. Use your imagination and you can usually think of a better way of getting the idea across — a way that won't be so confusing to your reader.

● anecdote

An *anecdote* is an interesting or humorous incident or story indirectly related to the writer's subject. You may have a boss who takes a dim view of using this device in formal writing or correspondence, in which case there may not be much you can do about it. The fact is, however, that many excellent writers use the device frequently, and to good advantage. A well-chosen anecdote can be very useful in developing or clarifying a difficult or obscure point.

● antecedent

Definition: The word, phrase, or clause to which a *relative pronoun* refers. The term *antecedent* literally means "going before." For example, in the sentence *My brother put on his coat,* the word *brother* is the antecedent of *his.*

Don't let the "going before" idea confuse you unduly. There are cases, not necessarily logical, but usually clear, in which the antecedent *follows* the pronoun. For example, *"After her severe fall, Mrs. Jones was never the same again."*

While we're on the subject, let me remind you that a pronoun must agree with its antecedent in *gender, number,* and *person.* Its *case,* however, is determined by its use with other words.

● anticipatory constructions (see expletives)

● anxious/eager

Careless writers often use these two words more or less interchangeably. They shouldn't. Use *anxious* only when you mean to communicate the idea of real anxiety, as "I am anxious about the lack of safety precautions." But *eager* is a better choice when you say something such as "I'm eager to meet the new boss."

● audience

Find out as much as you can about your intended audience before you begin to write. Perhaps I am exceptionally fussy about this because I spent so many years writing speeches. Even so, in other kinds of writing, the audience is *still* just as important a consideration.

If you are aiming at, say, a PTA group, you'll use different language, different structure, different illustrations, different almost everything from what you would use for, say, the members of a scientific or technical society.

If you're writing in response to a letter or a memo, you can usually learn quite a bit about your correspondent — just by reading carefully and with understanding. Is the writing formal or informal? How elaborate are the sentence structures? What kind of vocabulary is used? And so forth. Use the original correspondence for your cue; then be as responsive as you possibly can.

To sum up: *Slant your material to your audience.* If you don't have any clues, do this: imagine a reader that is intelligent, but perhaps not well informed on the particular subject you are writing about. Be simple and direct. Avoid complications. And whatever else you do, don't assume a pontifical or preachy tone that insults the reader's dignity or intelligence.

● avoidance — the merits of

If a sentence is hopelessly bad, don't spend the day trying to straighten it out. Just fall back and regroup. Rewrite the sentence *totally,* avoiding the problem instead of trying to wrestle with it. Using a little flexibility in your thinking can save you much time and heartache. I've used this example elsewhere in this handbook in another context, but it demonstrates extremely well what we might call the creative approach:

Rule 46 of the Oxford Union Society in London reads: *Any member introducing a dog into the Society's premises shall be liable to a fine of one pound. Any animal leading a blind person shall be deemed to be a cat.*

● bad/badly

Many otherwise careful writers and speakers apparently don't know the proper distinctions between this pair of words. *Bad* is an adjective; use it to follow such *linking verbs* as "feel" and "look." For example, you should say, "I felt bad about John's troubles last week."

Badly is an adverb. Use it to modify a verb, as in "The new equipment performed very badly until the mechanic repaired the control system."

Saying "I feel badly" would mean, if you take the expression in its literal sense, that your sense of touch doesn't work well.

● bi/semi

These are a couple of terms I wish we could do without — and many times we can. Most of the time they confuse the reader unduly. When you say, "The report comes out biweekly," do you mean it comes out twice a week, or every two weeks?

Well, ordinarily, when used with periods of time, *bi* means "two" or "every two." Thus, biweekly means "once every two weeks." Unfortunately, many writers don't use it this way.

When *semi* is used, it is supposed to mean "half of" or "occurring twice within the specified period of time." Thus, *semimonthly* should mean twice a month, and *semiweekly,* twice a week.

In my opinion, to avoid being misunderstood, you'd be a lot better off to say, "twice a week," or "twice a month," or whatever.

If you do ignore my advice and use the terms, remember that they both should normally be joined to the word following them without space or hyphen.

● biannual/biennial

According to the conventions of English usage, *biannual* means twice during a single year, and *biennial* means once every other year. I dislike this usage intensely — it is undoubtedly confusing to many readers. Why not say *semiannual* to indicate twice yearly? (That's the term we used at NASA to title our twice-yearly report to Congress: *The Semiannual Report.* There was still a problem, though, when the report fell a year or two behind schedule!)

● brief

A *brief* is a condensed statement of a long document or a series of documents. (In law, a brief is a statement filed by an attorney before arguing a case in court, but we're not concerned with that special meaning here.) Frequently you can help the reader, particularly when you're introducing a long piece of writing, if you give a quick summary of the contents at the beginning. This saves time and aids comprehension by giving a bird's eye view. (Sometimes the words *brief* and *abstract* are used as synonyms, although technically there are differences.)

At times you may find it necessary to furnish a boiled-down version of a report or article. If you're a staff member, you'll be called upon to brief your superiors; that is what most people think of when *briefing* is mentioned. However, writers can use essentially the same techniques to write a *summary* or *abstract* of a report.

The ability to do a good briefing doesn't come naturally. You'll have to work at it. But here are some tips on the most important things you will need to know. They are adapted freely from *Writing Guide for Naval Officers, NAVPERS 10009-A,* no longer in print.

SEVEN STEPS TO EXPEDITE A BRIEF

1. Read the entire report to determine the scope and point of view. If the material is difficult, study it until you are sure of the main ideas.

2. Underline important sentences or phrases in each paragraph. The underlined material should tell what the paragraph is about. Avoid asides and extras, but retain all major thoughts.

3. Write the underlined sentences or phrases in the order in which they appear. As far as possible, keep the author's emphasis and his original plan of organization. (In a resume, abstract, or paraphrase, you summarize in your own words and therefore often change the order. In a *brief,* you follow the author's order of presentation.)

4. Condense by eliminating unessential words and phrases, by substituting one sentence to do the work of two or three, by discarding illustrations and anecdotes, and by making generalizations to cover such data as statistics.

5. Put the author's material in your own words — if this helps the condensation. Use easy words and simple sentence structure. Don't put too many ideas into too tight a package. A style that is too clipped makes for hard reading. Make your sentences complete, and don't leave out verbs.

6. Show relationship of ideas by transitions. Tie the material together so that the reader can progress easily from one idea to the next. A series of short, unrelated statements makes stumbling reading.

7. Judge the length of your summary by the needs of the user. You may have to write and rewrite in order to satisfy the user's requirements and still show the author's intent.

● bureaucrats

This definition, by the brilliant and very funny James H. Boren, is too good to leave out: *Bureaucrats are the only people in the world who can say absolutely nothing and mean it.*

As a member of the bureaucracy for 27 years, I think I can take just as much pride in that definition as all the rest of you bureaucrats.

● can/may

In speech these days, few persons make any real distinction between these two words. Too bad, since the distinction is a useful one. In writing, please observe it if you want to be accurate. *Can* refers to capability, and *may* refers to possibility or permission. For example, you should say, "I can finish this job by this afternoon" to show capability. Say, "I may go to town Thursday" to show possibility; "I *can* go to town Thursday" to show capability. Use "May I go with you to the store" to ask permission.

● cause and effect (see organization)

● chairman/chairwoman/chairperson

Maybe my male chauvinism is apparent here, but I don't really believe so. The word *chairman* serves admirably for both sexes. If you trace the word back to its roots, the *man* part of the word comes from *Mann,* which encompassed both male and female. It was generic in the true sense. Thus, there is really no need to alter the word. If, however, you are still uncomfortable with this usage, why not simply say "Madam Chairman." That still sounds okay to most ears. Even *chairwoman* might not be too bad, although far from great. But *chairperson,* it seems to me, sounds terrible — really awful. Go ahead and use it if you feel you must, but not with my blessing.

Let's consider a few ramifications of this general problem. Back in the time of Amelia Earhart, we used to say "aviatrix." Nowadays, "aviator" works fine. Elizabeth Barrett Browning, Emily Dickinson, and Christina Rossetti were called "poetesses," although today we call them "poets." My point is, many words that once required special feminine endings no longer do, and many once masculine words now encompass both sexes. But — I repeat — such words as *chairman* have *always* applied to both sexes. So, for heaven's sake, let's not over-react! (For further discussion of sexism in language, see *he/she dilemma*.)

● chronological order (see organization)

● collective (collective noun)

In my seminars, I often try to explain this by the analogy of a hand in the form of a fist, as singular, or with separate fingers, plural. For example, *The committee is unanimous in its decision* is an obvious case where the collective noun *committee* is working as a single unit. But in the sentence *The membership are divided, with half wanting to secede and the rest wanting to stay,* the plural seems to be in order. The writer is the final judge in making these decisions. However, if you are in doubt, waffle. Write around the problem. You could say, for example, . . . *The members of the group disagree,* and the problem disappears. Don't sweat it.

One more thing. Whatever you do, be consistent.

● comma (see also punctuation)

The punctuation mark we call the *comma* is a tricky little devil, and current newspaper style is making it even trickier. For example, most newspapers do not put a comma before the final "and" in words or phrases in a series. This nefarious practice saves the typesetter from having to whack a lot of extra strokes on the typesetting machine. So who cares if the meaning is obscured in the process?

The question is rhetorical. Many writers care —and care very much. Strunk and White, for example, and another respected authority, Sheridan Baker (*The Practical Stylist*), are quite firm about this. Indeed, an impressively large and erudite group agrees that the comma before the *and* is important to clarity. Let's consider for a moment an actual example of the 'missing comma' usage we're all complaining about: *Write name, address, age, sex and housing requirements.*

For a complete discussion of commas, I must refer you to the authorities I've mentioned, or to many other excellent handbooks. Here I will simply give you four practical rules of thumb that cover most of the everyday problems you're likely to encounter:

1. Use commas between all words in a series, *including the last two,* unless you are considering the two as an inseparable pair, such as "ham and eggs."

2. Use a comma before conjunctions when joining independent clauses.

3. Enclose parenthetical insertions (see *restrictive and nonrestrictive*) with a pair of commas. Don't put a comma at one end of the insertion but not at the other.

4. Use a comma after an introductory phrase, to separate it from the rest of the sentence.

● compare/contrast

When you *compare* things, you usually point out both the similarities and the differences. When you *contrast,* you point out only the differences.

● compare to/compare with

You compare similar things *with* each other. You compare dissimilar things *to* each other.

Thus, you compare Marlene Dietrich *with* Gloria Swanson, but you compare an orange *to* a baseball.

● compose/comprise

These are a tricky pair, often confused. Remember that *comprise* contains the idea of "to include." Thus, the whole *comprises* the parts. *Compose,* on the other hand, means to "make up the whole." Thus, the parts *compose* the whole.

● congenial/genial

Somewhere along the way you've probably heard someone say, "She's a most congenial hostess." No way. The prefix *con-* means "with; together." Therefore, the hostess may indeed be marvelous, but she is just one person, so you shouldn't call her "congenial." If she is kindly, cordial, and all those other good things, call her "genial." Use *congenial* only when you're talking or writing about two or more individuals who are friendly or get along well together.

● context – taking material out of

Lawyers like to put everything including the kitchen sink in one sentence. Most lawyers, that is. They don't really seem to care if the sentence turns out to be several miles long. If you don't do things that way, they intone piously, someone will take a statement out of context.

Nonsense! Even the ten commandments were written one sentence at a time, and they have held up very well indeed for as long as any legal documents still extant.

My advice to you (and brace yourself, because members of your organization's legal staff may take issue) is *do not worry about being taken out of context*. Use the methodology outlined below. If you do, nobody can take anything out of context without being caught with egg on his face. (I used only the masculine form here because we know women would be too clever— and too honest — even to try such a thing.)

So, instead of trying to pack seventeen jillion facts (and ALL the exceptions) into one ridiculously long sentence, do things this way:

1. Say one thing in each sentence — don't pack in any extra information or thoughts.

2. If the stated idea must be qualified, *do so in the very next sentence.* It is a mistaken notion to think that all your qualifications and exceptions must be packaged within one single sentence.

3. Put the most important idea in each sentence at the beginning.

4. Use single words that mean essentially the same thing as phrases whenever you can. For example, instead of saying "persons who are residents of the State of Virginia," why not say, "residents of Virginia," or perhaps, "Virginia residents"?

5. Substitute everyday words for difficult words. If you *must* use technical or legalistic terms, be sure to define them. Give examples if necessary. Don't expect readers to have a lawyer's vocabulary!

6. Don't omit steps or take shortcuts in the belief that the reader will "obviously understand."

● copyright

If you are planning to write a report or a book for publication, and wish to quote material that has been copyrighted, here are a few things you ought to know:

1. Copyrighted material is literary property. If you "borrow" someone else's words, you must give credit where credit is due. This means simply that you will indicate the source of the material — the

name of the author, the name of the publication, and usually but not always, the page number. The standard "academic" way is to put this information in footnotes. To be more informal, you may enclose the information in parentheses. (I planned to use footnotes when I started writing this book. When I found out what a hassle it was in typesetting, I gave way to practicality. When you are doing typewritten pages, footnotes are fairly easy. When you're composing type, they are a pain.)

2. If you're planning to quote more than a few lines, you should formally request permission from the holder of the copyright. What is called "fair use" varies somewhat according to the kind of material. In prose, the standard practice is this: you can use up to about 150 words (in some cases, up to about 500, or so I'm told, but I'd play it safe and stick to the lower number) without asking formal permission. Also, if the paper you are writing won't be published or circulated in any way, you don't have to ask permission.

You can use most government documents published by the Government Printing Office (GPO) without having to get copyright permission. The reasoning is that the writing and printing were done at taxpayers' expense, and hence are public property.

In theory, you could "borrow" such material without even mentioning source or giving formal attribution. But it wouldn't be ethical — and it won't cost you a thing to identify your source.

Some government material *is* copyrighted. If it is, there will be a standard copyright notice up front.

You probably already are aware that the works of many great literary figures of the past are now in the public domain. That means simply this: if you want to pick up and use any of this material, you can borrow, quote, or misquote, with no fear of retribution. It still isn't exactly cricket to try to get away with copying a poem such as "How do I love thee, let me count the ways," and taking credit for the composition. (A character in a Peter DeVries novel did just that.) The problem is that there might be some readers around who recognize the language. Perhaps that possibility is all that keeps some writers honest. Who knows?

● **criteria/criterion**

Here is a troublesome pair of words that are frequently confused or misused. *Criteria* is plural. *Criterion* is singular. Pay attention. Don't use them interchangeably, as I have heard many persons do. It's bad enough to use them incorrectly, but to use them incorrectly *and* inconsistently is even worse!

● data/datum

Here we have another troublesome pair. In Latin, *data* is plural, *datum* is singular. In English, we find confusion. Some writers use *data* as singular, others use it as plural. The ones who use it as singular probably don't use *datum* at all — they may not even know the word. So, my advice to you is this: be consistent!

According to most good dictionaries, it is considered acceptable to use *data* as either a singular or a plural. Most scientists and engineers prefer the Latin usage. Just about everybody else likes it better the other way. So, take your choice, but stick to it.

● detail — need for attention to

THE CASE OF THE MISSING HYPHEN

When I was working at NASA in the early days of the space program, we had to think up quite a few synonyms for the word "failure." Murphy's Law was, and always is, especially tough on great technological projects at their beginnings. Things went wrong that you wouldn't believe. Jim Aswell and I spent days thinking up new ways to say in our reports that, "although the launch vehicle blew up on the pad, we gained much valuable information from the experiment."

Years later, when the launch record was much, much better, the then NASA Administrator, James E. Webb, asked Jim and me to put together a collection of motion picture film clips. He used this footage to illustrate speeches about the progress of the space program. The film started with 90 seconds of rockets blowing up in all kinds of horrible ways; I can still see them in my dreams.

Mr. Webb was willing to show the failures because eventually our engineers and technicians came as close to achieving perfection as did any organization in all history. Those of us who were there were proud of the accomplishments — and still are.

Still, there were occasional glitches to keep us humble. Once NASA launched a communications satellite that went into orbit, but no one could talk to it. Another time a probe to Mars or Venus (I forget which) didn't do what it was supposed to do because a programmer left out a single "hyphen" in the programming instructions.

A high NASA official won my undying admiration when he hung prominently in his office a large oil painting: a beautifully white square of canvas with a small, very black hyphen in the middle.

I needn't point out the moral, but I'll do it anyway. When you are dealing with difficult subjects — anything from telling a space probe what to do while on its way to another planet to telling a harrassed parent how to assemble a bicycle on Christmas Eve — you can't be too careful about your language.

Most instructions that come with knockdown furniture, kits of various kinds, and similar inventions of the devil appear to be written as if the writer wanted to make sure the reader couldn't possibly understand. If indeed that is the intention, the rate of success is far higher than we ever achieved at NASA in our most halcyon days.

● diction

This is a word that you may faintly recall having heard your English teacher use. You can doubtless get along quite well without knowing the word, but not without a knowledge of the problem it defines — namely, the choice of words in any type of communication, especially in regard to correctness, clarity, or effectiveness.

Teachers of college courses in composition constantly rail at students with cries of "Faulty diction." That's just their way of saying that a student has used a word improperly, or has used a "non-standard" word in a formal paper.

● direct object (see sentence — the parts of)

● draft — getting it down on paper

There are occasions when you don't want to stop and hunt for the exact word you need (what we've called earlier, the *mot juste.)* One of the more common such occasions is that of writing a first draft. You have probably discovered it doesn't pay to stop and hunt for a word because you're likely to lose your trend of thought.

Your instincts are correct. Just put your idea down fast. Don't hesitate, and don't worry about "style," whatever that is. Go ahead and use the wrong word, or a roundabout phrase if you need to — so long as you can keep the idea going. You can come back for the exact word later. (I've heard of writers who just put down an illegible scrawl to represent a word they can't think of. Psychologically, that might be a good trick.)

Let me emphasize — *don't pause. Get the idea down on paper.* Edit it later. You'll be glad, because that way you'll have some copy to edit. That certainly beats staring at a blank sheet of paper.

● due to/because of

Back in the olden days, my major professor gave me hell for using "due to" in my thesis when I should have used "because of." If I had done it today, I might have been able to get away with it, although careful writers should still observe the distinction. *Due to* means "caused by" and can be used properly to follow a *linking verb*. For example, you could say, "His tired appearance was due to overwork." Many writers, however, would still consider "due to" to be unacceptable when used with a nonlinking verb to replace *because of*. I suggest that you watch the distinctions, but have to admit that not too many readers know or care about the difference these days.

● each other/one another

No need to be confused, although many writers are. When you are referring to a relationship between two persons, say *each other*. When you are referring to more than two, say *one another*. Once you understand the difference, it's easy to keep these straight.

●elegant variation

Some writers will go to any extreme to avoid repeating a word within some arbitrary measure, usually (but not always) a paragraph. They will substitute farfetched synonyms, often pretentious ones, instead of simply repeating the word. This amateurish practice is called *elegant variation*. (I believe Fowler coined the term.) A simple word like *letter* becomes an *epistle* the next time it turns up, then perhaps a *missive,* a *note,* or a *written communication.*

Sometimes this practice is annoying but harmless. But it can be not only bad, but dangerous, when you are writing regulations or instructions. If you say something such as *car* one place, *vehicle,* the next, and *automobile,* the next, you may have demonstrated the breadth of your vocabulary, but you have also probably bewildered the reader. *Don't do it.* Repeat key words as often as necessary for clarity. Your readers will love you for it.

Sports writers are particularly fond of this device, to the point of frivolity: Ohio *belts* Minnesota; Illinois *buries* Purdue; Pittsburgh *shocks* Indiana; Harvard *thumps* Yale — and so on, ad nauseam. Apparently, the writers are having a ball, but a little of this goes a long way. Don't try your readers' patience.

emphasis — word placement for

If you intend to put particular emphasis on a word or phrase, you have two options: you can put the important information at the very beginning, or at the very end.

Strunk and White say putting things at the end is better. For *literary* writing, which is what they're talking about, they're probably right. But for "useful" writing, the advantages of placing the emphatic material at the end may be outweighed by other factors. Your reader needs to know the direction you're taking as soon as possible — otherwise there can be confusion or misinterpretation.

Accordingly — at least in most cases — you'll probably get your emphatic points across more clearly and accurately by putting them up front. That goes — hard to believe — even for *conclusions.* Granted that conclusions are supposed to conclude. Go ahead and do it that way, but give the reader a preview. Like just about everything else I tell you, this "rule" isn't a rule, and sometimes it doesn't work. Try the simple trick of writing the information both ways, if you're in doubt. Then you can see which method communicates most clearly and emphatically.

exposition

You hear a great deal in college composition classes about something called "Exposition." In the real world, you can probably get through life without ever having to use the term, or certainly, to define it. But just to make sure we are taking advantage of all your previous training in composition, let's pause for a brief reminder.

Exposition is one of four basic forms of communication that you usually bump up against in English Comp I. For workaday writers, including thee and me, exposition is far more important than any of the other three forms. (For the record, the other three are *narration, description,* and *argumentation,* including *persuasion.*)

Probably the most common, efficient, and generally useful pattern of exposition is the *example* or *analogy.* We use these very naturally in speech; we should try to do the same in writing. Instead of talking in generalities about the qualities of a good football coach, we cite Vince Lombardi or Don Schula or George Allen. We may build an even stronger and better word picture for our readers by going a step further — we could illustrate our chosen coach's outstanding abilities by giving a specific account of his handling of a crucial situation in the playoffs or the Superbowl or whatever. Elsewhere in this handbook I give you an impassioned dissertation on the advantages of using concrete rather than abstract illustrations. Do that any time you can, for you will automatically increase clarity by so doing. You'll also get increased reader interest at the same time. This is extremely important: clear writing isn't much help if it puts your reader to sleep. (I seem to recall having said that before. Oh well, it bears repeating.)

Dr. Isaac Asimov, who in my opinion — and his too — is far and away America's best writer when it comes to explaining difficult concepts in clear language, is a bearcat at giving examples and analogies. He often does this so well that I can read one of his explanations and go around for·awhile thinking I understand Einstein's theory and other good stuff like that.

● expletive

An *expletive* is a word that fills the position or takes the place of another word, phrase, or clause. The ones we use most frequently are "there is" and "there are." Sometimes such constructions are helpful to avoid awkwardness, but usually they are just fillers, a waste of words. Avoid them if you can. Instead of writing, for example, "There were many members present," write "Many members were present."
NOTE: Do not confuse this kind of *expletive* with the other definition of the term — that is, the "expletive deleted" of Watergate fame!

● familiar words — use of

One of the most important rules in useful writing is *Prefer the familiar word to the farfetched.* Here are a few samples I've collected that show you how *not* to do it:

> In order to avoid negative reflections as a result of dysfunctional internal communications, and in order to enhance the possibilities of coordinated balances, I am strongly urging that any item having a direct or indirect affect [sic] on the NW No. 1 Project Area be made known to me before, rather than after, it's [sic] occurrence, when possible.
> —Memo written by an official of the D.C. Redevelopment Land Agency

> Sign at entrance to a corridor in the Pentagon:
> THIS PASSAGEWAY HAS BEEN MADE NONCONDUCIVE TO UTILIZATION FOR AN INDEFINITE PERIOD
> — Quoted in *The Kidner Report,* p. 55

● files

Build up files on every subject you might conceivably be writing about. Make them as complete as you can. If you run across an article that might be useful, clip it and stow it in an appropriately labeled file folder. (That last is really important. It's no good if you can't find it. Don't put off organizing. Keep on doing it as you go along.)

When I was chief of the ghostwriting group at NASA Headquarters, I was spoiled in this regard. We had secretaries and research assistants to help us keep things organized and sorted out. With their help, we managed to fill half a dozen big file cabinets with material on every conceivable phase of the aeronautics and space program. These beautifully organized files came to our rescue many times when we would get a call at 8:30 a.m. to deliver a finished speech that afternoon. (Don't think such things didn't happen. They did — far too often. That's one of the reasons I'm glad to be out of the ghostwriting business.)

Nowadays I must do my own clipping and filing. Huge stacks of clippings and papers cover every bit of table and chair space in sight. I know that what I am looking for is in there someplace, but I haven't the faintest idea where. Then, by Murphy's Law, I get a short-fuse writing assignment and have to stay up half the night tracking down the items I need.

So, I suggest that you do what I *say* on this matter, not what I *do*.

● first person singular — the "perpendicular pronoun"

Some organizations and agencies have a rule that nobody but the top boss uses the "perpendicular pronoun." It may sound arbitrary, but maybe they're right. Most of us may be writing on behalf of an organization, and very likely are not calling the shots. This doesn't mean you must avoid personal pronouns entirely. Many times, the plural form, "we," will work just fine. Putting the emphasis on "you" is often even better, but even that can be overdone.

The trick is to place yourself in the background, so that the writing doesn't emerge as a continuing ego trip. As one of my heroes, E. B. White, puts it: "Write in a way that draws the reader's attention to the substance of the writing, rather than to the mood and temper of the author." (*The Elements of Style, p. 62.*)

● flags (queries)

Many times, when editing, you will encounter sentences that can be interpreted in any of several different ways. You know that you want to edit the sentence so that the correct interpretation is the only one possible. You may believe you know exactly which interpretation is correct, but you can't always be sure. What do you do?

You can ask the originator to explain the intended meaning, and then rewrite the sentence accordingly. That's easy if the writer is in the next office, or just down the hall. But, suppose the originator is clear across the country. You don't want to waste time and money by making a long-distance call every time you have a question.

Many of the good editors I know use the device called a "flag" — or sometimes, a "query." It comes as close to being a foolproof way of handling these difficult situations as you are likely to find. Take it in steps, like this:

1. Using all the logic and information you have at your command, make an "educated guess." Chances are good that you will come up with the correct intent of the ambiguous sentence.

2. Rewrite the sentence very carefully, the way you think it should be, to reflect the intent you consider correct. Make sure that the rewrite is itself not open to several interpretations.

3. Put in a "flag." That is to say, write the word FLAG in big capital letters, underscored, as near as you can to the place on the page where you have made your editorial change. After the word FLAG, query the originator about the problem. Call attention to your change and invite the originator's opinion of your rewrite.

This may sound complicated, but if you leave the sentence as it was with a "query" in the margin indicating your confusion, there's a good chance the author won't even recognize what your problem is. Since familiarity blinds us to our own words, the author will think the original statement perfectly clear. But if you rewrite the offending sentence carefully you will illuminate the problem, even if — as is quite possible — you may choose exactly the opposite meaning from the one intended.

When you rewrite, don't forget the FLAG in the margin. Without it the author, in looking over your rewrite, may not notice the change. But I guarantee you it will leap off the page of the printed version. And that's when the author will call you on the carpet.

● footnotes

Footnotes can be very helpful devices for both writer and reader. They enable the writer to keep the narrative going full tilt without having to put in material that would slow things down. But the information is still there, in footnote form, for anyone who wants it.

Readers are happy, because if they are interested primarily in the narrative, they can read straight through. If, on the other hand, they are concerned with minute details, those too are readily and handily available. Writer and reader share the best of all possible worlds.

But footnotes should be used properly, and located properly. One of my pet peeves is the method used by many publishers — the method of putting all the footnotes, bunched together, at the end of a chapter, or worse — clear at the end of the book. This leaves the reader with several choices, all miserable. One choice involves reading through the chapter and then going back and reading the footnotes. This is bad because the reader forgets what the footnotes are referring to. The alternative is just as bad — flipflopping back and forth between the text and the footnotes — an extremely time-consuming operation.

Incidentally, a properly used footnote can be useful in ways that might not ordinarily occur to you. If you're trying to impress the boss, or your colleagues, don't forget footnotes. Those of you who have written scholarly papers, or a thesis or dissertation, know that footnotes can add an impressively academic looking appearance to the most ordinary manuscript. Academic illiterates will compose great tangled jungles of jargon, sprinkle in a few *Ibids* and *op. cits.,* and their stupidities take on a protective coloration that makes them much harder to recognize.

Seriously — the footnote device can offer you real benefits. Suppose, for example, you're writing along, everything is going well, and you have worked up a good head of steam. Then you feel a need to put in material with a degree of detail that some readers will want to know, but others won't care a thing about. Take my advice — put the extra detail in a footnote, and you'll be able to satisfy both groups. And that's a really worthwhile trick.

But — I plead with you — don't ever put explanatory footnotes anywhere except on the same page or pages with the material they refer to. (Documentation is a different matter. It's okay to list authors, references, and the like, at the end, if this will be easier for the production staff.)

● future tense

Future tense usually is not much of a problem in writing, but upon occasion, some of my seminar students have questioned such constructions as "Tomorrow is Monday." They ask, "Shouldn't we say, 'Tomorrow will be Monday'?"

Well, it is okay to say that if you want to, but it really is not at all necessary. "Tomorrow" expresses all the futurity you need.

If you use the idiom of the American language comfortably, as I hope you do, you shouldn't be bothered at this idiomatic expression. If some literal-minded soul says you should say "Tomorrow will be Monday," a bit of ear training is in order.

● fuzzify

I'm putting this term in because I find it irresistible. It was coined by the perceptive and witty James H. Boren. (Dr. Boren is the creator of such slogans as "When in doubt, mumble," and "If you are going to be a phony, be sincere about it.") He defines the term "fuzzify" as *the presentation of a matter in terms that permit adjusive interpretation. Particularly useful when the fuzzifier does not know what he or she is talking about, or when the fuzzifier wants to enunciate a non-position in the form of a position.*

The non-Boren word for this is "waffling," but I don't like it nearly so well.

● grammar — a few elementary principles

nouns — Words used to denote persons, places, or things, are called nouns. Thus the words *man, woman, child, train, city,* are nouns. Nouns are also used as the names of qualities or ideas, such as *patriotism, kindness, happiness, truth,* and *love.*

Common nouns name members of a class of persons, places, or things, such as *dog, country, chair.*

Proper nouns name particular persons, places, or things (*Jimmy Carter, Maryland, Brooklyn Bridge).* Begin a proper noun with a capital letter.

pronouns — In the sentence *The woman saw the little girl but did not speak to her,* the word *her* is used instead of *girl.* A word used to take the place of a noun is called a *pronoun.* Pronouns, as well as nouns, are used as *subjects* or *direct objects.*

The word the pronoun refers to is called its *antecedent.* In the sentence given above, *girl* is the antecedent of *her.*

Pronouns are divided into various classes. The pronouns *I, you, he, she, it, we,* and *they* are called *personal* pronouns.

When *who, which,* and *what* are used to introduce questions they are called *interrogative* pronouns. When they are used in sentences that are not questions they are called *relative* pronouns. Thus, in the sentence *Who gave you the money?* the word *who* is an interrogative pronoun. In the sentence *It was my brother who gave me the money,* the word *who* is a relative pronoun.

number —We have different forms of nouns and pronouns to show whether we are referring to one person or thing or to more than one. Thus *I* refers to one person, *we* refers to more than one. This distinction is called *number. I* is in the *singular* number, and *we* is in the *plural* number. In the same way, *horse* is in the singular number, and *horses* is in the plural number.

case — Such pronouns as *he, she,* and *who* have different forms to show how they are used in sentences. We say *She walks, I see her,* and *I have his tickets.* In these sentences, *she* is a subject, *her* is a direct object, and *his* refers to a person possessing something. In like manner, we use *she* and *who* as subjects, *her* and *whom* as direct objects of a verb or as objects of a preposition, and *her (*or *hers)* and *whose* to denote the person possessing something.

A noun has the same form for the subject as for the object of a verb or a preposition, but it has a different form to refer to a person as possessing something. Thus we say *The man walks, I see the man, I have the man's hat.* These different forms and uses of nouns and pronouns in sentences are called — in "traditional" English grammar — *cases.* The subject is in the *nominative* case, the direct object is in the *objective* case (sometimes called the *accusative* as a holdover from Latin grammar), and the word referring to the possessor is in the *possessive* case (the *genitive* in Latin grammar).

direct objects — As just explained in the previous entry, a noun or pronoun must be in the *objective* (or *accusative*) case when it receives the action of a *transitive verb.*

indirect object — A noun or pronoun used to denote the person to whom something is given, said, or shown is termed an *indirect object.* In the sentences *He gave my brother an apple* and *My sister told me the news,* the words *brother* and *me* are indirect objects. NOTE: Phrases with "to" are sometimes equivalent to indirect objects. Instead of saying *I gave John the letter,* we may express the same idea by saying *I gave the letter to John.* In the second version, *to John* takes the place of the indirect object *John* in the first.

verbs — In the sentences *The man runs* and *The panther leaped,* the words *runs* and *leaped* denote actions. Such words are called *verbs.* Some verbs denote mere existence or continuance in place rather than action. In the sentences *John is in the kitchen,* and *We shall remain here until noon,* we see examples of this usage.

person and number of verbs — In some tenses, a verb has a different form when its subject is in the first person (*I, we*) from what it would have if the subject were in the third person (*he, she, it, they*). Thus we say *I walk,* but *he walks.* The third person plural also differs from the third person singular. Thus, *he walks, she walks, it walks, they walk.* A verb is said to be in the same *person* and *number* as its subject.

transitive and intransitive verbs — A verb that takes a *direct object* is called a *transitive verb.* In the sentence *John saw the movie,* the verb *saw* is transitive. A verb that does not take a direct object is called an *intransitive verb.* In the sentence *The prisoner wept,* the verb *wept* is intransitive. However, if the sentence were changed to *The prisoner wept bitter tears,* the verb *wept* would be transitive.

I should mention here, and probably should have mentioned elsewhere, that only *transitive* verbs can have either an *active* or a *passive* form.

adjectives — We often use some other word with a noun to tell about — or to *modify* — the noun. Thus, in the expressions *tall buildings* and *red paint,* the words *tall* and *red* tell something about the buildings and the paint. Such words are called *adjectives.*

Adjectives that merely indicate what is being referred to without suggesting quality are *this, that, other, same.* The adjectives *the, a,* and *an* also belong in this class, but are called *articles.*

Predicate adjectives are used after *linking verbs* (such as *is, was, were,* etc.) and refer back to the subject.

conjunctions — The words *and, but,* and *or* (or *nor*) are used to join words or parts of sentences. In the sentence *Your brothers and sisters are away from home,* the word *and* is used to join *brothers* and *sisters.*

Subordinating conjunctions are such words as *although, because, if, after, where, than, since, as, unless, before, that, though, when,* and *whereas.* These join subordinate phrases (or clauses) to the main statement of a sentence, as in *The road is good, although it is narrow.*

prepositions — There is a class of small words such as *of, in, with, by, from,* which are used with nouns or pronouns. The combination of one of these words and the noun or pronoun it is used with serves to tell something about an act or about a person or thing. These words are called *prepositions.* The noun or pronoun that follows a preposition is called its *object,* or the preposition is said to *govern* the noun or pronoun that follows it. In the sentence *I live in Fairfax,* the word *Fairfax* is the object of *in.*

● handles

Indexes are great, but many publications can't or don't use them for one reason or another. How else can you give your readers a "handle" on the material, making it easier for them to track down the specific information they seek? Here are a few suggestions:

- Use titles and subtitles, headings and subheadings
- Use checklists, breakdowns, summaries, and similar devices
- Use references and cross-references; use underscores or other typographical devices to call attention to important ideas or key words.
- Make the Table of Contents more than just a chapter listing. Give headings and subheadings as well.
- Furnish a table of figures and illustrations. (Make sure that these illustrations are on the same page as the describing text, or at least on a facing page.)
- Make use of alphabetical or numerical arrangements that readers can easily follow.

● he/she dilemma (sexism in language)

Have you noticed — and I hope you haven't, because if you have I haven't been nearly as slick as I have hoped — throughout this book I have conscientiously strained every nerve to avoid using a single sexist construction. (This may be the first book ever written by a male chauvinist pig to make that claim.) If I've failed it has been through oversight, not design. Mind you, I'm not responsible for quotations from other sources — just my own writing.

Now that I have openly announced my intent, perhaps you can skim through and detect some of the devices I've employed. To help your search, I'll spell out a few:

1. Use a plural subject when the situation permits. This will permit you to use "their" grammatically when you refer to the antecedent.

EXAMPLE: Instead of saying "Any employee who will not reach *his* or *her* 40th birthday before . . ." try saying "Any employees who will not reach *their* . . ."

2. Refer to the person's job title or organizational position, making no reference to the sex of the individual holding the job.

EXAMPLE: Instead of saying "The girl at the reception desk will give you directions," say "The receptionist will give you directions." (NOTE: The new directory of occupational job titles is a big help.

Sexist titles such as *Fireman* or *stewardess* have been changed to *firefighter* and *flight attendant*.)

3. Use your imagination to "write around" the pronoun.

EXAMPLE: Instead of writing "The promotion must come because the employee himself has worked to qualify for it," try something like "The promotion must come from the employee's own efforts to qualify . . ."

4. Use a slash between the two gender-related pronouns, if you can't think of any other way to handle it.

EXAMPLE: "Each participant must furnish his/her own documentation." (Even in this case, I think that using the plural "participants" would be better. But, of course, sometimes the plural simply is not accurate or appropriate — especially in regulations.)

Above all, bear in mind that with a bit of care and a small amount of imagination, writers can almost always "write around" the problem. This book is intended, among other things, to prove that point. I hope (not *hopefully*) that it has succeeded.

Before we leave this subject, however, one more point needs to be made. (See also the entry under *Chairman/Chairwoman/Chairperson)*

Where I truly feel it's necessary to draw the line is at the awkward words and constructions that bend our whole beautiful English language out of shape. Regretfully, I must point out that the indiscriminate use of *person* is a case in point. A recent *Washington Post* editorial (September 28, 1977) demonstrates very clearly the problem we're up against here. The editorial stated that the following utterance had appeared in a Presidential Proclamation: "The United States is a young Nation, but our debt to that courageous *Norseperson,* Leif Ericson, predates 1776 . . ." [emphasis added.]

The editorialist went on to say: "Our problem with this bizarre locution is not just that Leif Ericson, God rest his bones, would certainly have hated it. Nor is it merely the fact that Leif Ericson was a *Norseman,* as distinct, let us say, from a Norsewoman or a Norsechild. No, our concern is with the Big Picture, the pattern and precedent that this usage could easily establish."

The editorialist (incidentally, there's a good example of a nonsexist job title) makes the point that you can carry this "person" business to ridiculous extremes. "[Speaking of the Normans] . . . should we say Norperson and Norpersondy? And once you start down that road, why stop there?"

Surely that's enough to make the point. Hurray for the Women's Movement, but let's not get carried away.

● hopefully

This word, used correctly, means *with hope.* For example, *The beggar looked hopefully at the well-dressed stranger.*

Several months ago I attended a convention of the International Platform Association, where I heard some of the best (or at least the highest-paid) speakers in America. Virtually every speaker on the program used the word *hopefully* to mean *I hope* or *It is hoped.* So this is probably a lost cause. While "hopefully" we will stamp out this usage in the way I've just employed it, there are two chances, as Redd Foxx would say: slim and none.

Nevertheless, it is a sloppy and incorrect usage, and many careful writers are still concerned with making the appropriate distinction. As Bill Gold wrote in one of his columns: ' . . I hope, one hopes, it is to be hoped that today's speakers and writers will avoid misusing the word." ("The District Line," *The Washington Post,* May 5, 1977.)

One final comment. I heartily agree with Jean Stafford, a member of the Morrises' usage committee. She has a sign on her back door that reads: *The word "hopefully" must not be misused on these premises. Violators will be humiliated.*

● hyphen

The hyphen (-) is a very tricky punctuation mark. Many otherwise confident writers throw up their hands in dismay when confronted with the choice of using a hyphen or leaving it out. Fowler, in his *Modern English Usage,* devoted many pages of elaborate discussion to the subject, and then frankly admitted that many of the policies he prescribed wouldn't always work in actual practice. If that great expert of experts had so much trouble, what are the rest of us going to do?

I don't propose to solve all your problems. I'll just give you a few basic rules of thumb. (Some people would hyphenate that, rules-of-thumb.) Even those are subject to argument. My editor at Acropolis and I have strong differences of opinion. Since this is *my* book, I hope to win, but don't count on it. So far I've won a few and lost a few.

My first "rule" is that two-word (or sometimes three-word or four-word) *modifiers* that express a single thought should be hyphenated when they precede a noun. For example, an *out-of-order* machine, or a *state-of-the-art* component. The trick is to see whether the individual words can be used to modify the noun, or whether they must be used all together, as an entity. Thus, it wouldn't be an *out* or an *of* or an *order* machine — it has to be all three locked together. If each of the words could modify the noun without the aid of the other modifying word or words, you should *not* use a hyphen. Also, if the first word of the group is an adverb ending in *-ly*, do *not* use a hyphen. (NOTE: Most *non* prefixes do not require a hyphen. If you are in doubt, look it up.)

Early in this book, I started a sentence with the phrase *Well-crafted writing*. That one stirred up a hornet's nest. Some of the writers and editors I asked to read my manuscript said that well-crafted should be hyphenated. Others said that *well* was an adverb modifying crafted, and thus should *not* be hyphenated. I expect to be racked up by somebody, either way. That's the risk you take if you have the temerity to write a book on writing!

The next rule is this: when the modifying words *follow* the noun, do *not* hyphenate. For example, "Our writing textbooks are hopelessly *out of date.*" (No hyphens.)

● i.e.

The abbreviation *i.e.* stands for the Latin *id est,* meaning *that is.* Why not simply say "that is"? In my experience, many readers don't have the faintest idea what *i.e.* means.

NOTE: My friend Allan Lefcowitz (author of *The Writer's Handbook*) disagrees. He believes we should use *i.e.* and give readers a chance to learn something new,

● Indefinite pronoun

Definition: a pronoun that does not specify a person — *anyone, each, either, everyone, none, someone.* When such words are used to modify nouns, they are called *indefinite adjectives.* All except neither and *none* take a singular verb when followed by the preposition *of* and a plural noun. EXAMPLE: Each of the members was consulted.

NOTE: In recent years, many good writers have come to accept the plural verb. In such cases, a plural pronoun must follow. *Each of the members were consulted, and they agreed to have another election.*

● indirect object (see sentence — the parts of)

● inoperative

Ron Ziegler is gone. Let's send this miserable bit of jargon right along with him.

● infinitives — including the splitting thereof

Recently I was teaching a seminar at a large government agency, and one of the participants asked, "What is a split infinitive? We've been ordered not to split any, but I'm not sure what it is we're not supposed to split!"

Many writers share that problem. For the best discussion I know of on this subject, try Fowler's *Modern English Usage.* You'll find it not only enlightening but entertaining. First, he divides the English-speaking world into five categories, starting with (1) those who don't know what a split infinitive is, and don't care. Then he takes you through other categories, such as (2) those who don't know, but care very much; (3) those who know and approve, going miles out of the way to split infinitives at every opportunity; (4) those who know and condemn (and this category includes the head of the agency where the question arose); and (5) those who know and distinguish.

I've taken a few liberties with Fowler's language, I'm sure, since I'm playing this back from memory, but this is close enough to give you the idea. Furthermore, I *do* want you to look up the original.

If you don't, however, let me give you a very quick treatment:

An *infinitive* is a form of the verb that is proceeded by the *sign of the infinitive,* the preposition *to.* For example, *to go, to walk, to talk, to swim,* etc.

Because the *to* and the rest of the infinitive go together, many writers believe they should not be separated, or "split." Thus, a split infinitive consists of an infinitive in which a word or words (usually an adverb or an adverbial phrase) has been inserted, thus: to *quickly* walk, to *loudly* talk, etc.

In truth, speakers and writers have been splitting infinitives for hundreds of years. The Bard himself split a great many, one time or another. Still, the practice offends many readers, so my advice to you is to avoid splitting whenever you can. (And candidly, that's most of the time, if you practice the art of avoidance, discussed elsewhere.) Sheridan Baker, whom I admire, says you should *never* split an infinitive. Strunk and White, Fowler, and a long list of others will advise you to avoid splitting if you can. They do, however, say that splitting is acceptable if it results in improved clarity. I'll cheerfully go along with that — couldn't ask for better company.

● intensive (or intensifier)

An *intensifier* is an adverb that emphasizes degree, such as *quite, rather, such, too,* and *very* (last but *very* far from least — emphasis added to make the point). Sometimes a writer really needs and wants an intensifier. Such words can occasionally serve a legitimate and useful function. But they can also sneak up on you.

Most of us use far too many. I'm quite sure I do. (Oops! As I have just demonstrated, I'm not always successful at weeding them out.) So be on your guard. My mentor, Jim Aswell, always said the language would be better off if words such as *very* were totally wiped out. That pronouncement is severe, but Jim is probably — as he usually is — more right than wrong. Bash out the intensifiers unless they are clearly necessary, and you'll strengthen your writing.

●"ize" endings

We've discussed at length the wickedness known as "smothered verbs" — changing verbs into nouns by adding such endings as *-tion, -ization,* and *-ance.* (I haven't put a separate discussion of the subject in this Handbook Section because of the lengthy treatment in Chapter Three.) But little or nothing has been said so far about another crime that is almost as bad — the reverse situation in which nouns are changed to verbs — usually long and awkward verbs — by adding an "ize" ending. Admittedly, this device can sometimes be handy, or even useful. But, because it is easy to do, it can easily be overdone. "Ize" endings seem to be a constant source of temptation to many otherwise careful writers.

Let me call once more upon *The Kidner Report,* which gives us a wise and witty discussion on the subject:

> "ize" is used to add weight to a verb, or to convert a noun to a verb, thereby giving a prod to some pretty slow moving sentences. Bureaucracy never utilizes use when utilize can be utilized. It also totalizes, rarely does it total. *It systematizes; it seldom arranges. Programs are prioritized.*
>
> The approach to "ize-ing" is uncomplicated. Simply select a word that's been "ized" already and use it; or pick an "un-ized" word and "ize." The penultimate of the "ize" approach was reached by an Army colonel who, upon finding a project that would get along without many managers, *deproject-managerized* the whole thing. Logically, then, to undo any resulting catastrophe, one could easily *non-deprojectmanager-ize it.*

For those of you who are sufficiently entranced to want to read the rest of this brilliant dissertation, you can find it on page 45 of *The Kidner Report.* We can learn a great deal from Mr. Kidner's gentle (and sometimes not so gentle) kidding.

● jargon

Many editors will tell you to weed out jargon, and most of the time they're right. But not always. As you probably know, *jargon* is the technical language used by persons in the same field to communicate with one another. Over the years, these specialists have developed technical terms that mean precisely what they want them to mean. Thus, by using a single word of jargon, a specialist can often convey information to a colleague that might have required whole sentences, or even paragraphs, to communicate in the less exact language of nonspecialists in the field. So, rather than *eliminate jargon,* the "rule" should be *use jargon only when such language is appropriate to the reader.* After all, you shouldn't really have to care whether a layman can understand it if a layman isn't going to have to read it.

● layout

Proper layout of your copy can be a big help to your readers. Use every device you can — headings, subheadings, paragraph indentions, and so on. Even "white space" can be useful — nothing discourages a reader more than page after page of solid, close-set type, with nothing to relieve the monotony. Even if the writing itself is clear, its appearance is formidable.

illustrations — Give your readers the information they need *where they need it.* If you use an illustration or a table to go with an item in the text, put it on the very same page if you have room. Put it on a facing page if you don't. Please don't do what so many publishers are doing these days: gathering *all* the illustrations in one bundle and printing them together, usually right in the middle of the book. That way, they make the illustrations essentially useless. Readers either skip them entirely, or look at them all at once without reference to the text.

footnotes — Another evil trick is to put footnotes in a group at the end of the book, rather than on the same pages with the material they document. Any time a reader has to suffer this miserable flipflop back and forth from one end of the book to the other, the effectiveness of your communication diminishes accordingly.

Again, the problems of footnotes in printed material can be difficult. I started out thinking I would use footnotes, and when I found out how severe the typesetting problems would be, I threw up my hands and said "Forget it!" But most of you readers will be dealing primarily with type*writing,* not type*setting.* It is quite easy to handle footnotes in a typed manuscript. One way you might try is to put in footnotes right at the point they are needed — in the middle of a page, if necessary — and separate them from the text by a solid underscore line, clear across the page, above and below the footnote.

Check with your organization style manual. In many organizations this kind of arrangement is not prohibited, and I have found it is usually totally acceptable to readers.

forms — You may never be concerned with designing a form. If you are lucky, your organization will have trained professionals to perform this difficult and often thankless task, much better than you are likely to be able to do it. But the time may come when you'll have to do it yourself. Should this catastrophe ever befall you, keep the following guidelines in mind:

1. Be careful in designing and laying out the lines. How many forms have you seen lately that don't indicate clearly whether to put the required information *above* or *below* the line. The Virginia Driver's License is an example of how *not* to do it. You have to read clear to the bottom before you can figure it out. The only way to get things right is to start at the end and work backward.

2. Make sure the steps are presented in a logical order. If the person using the form needs certain information before answering other questions, follow an appropriate progression.

3. Make sure the lines are laid out to fit typewriter spacing — if, that is, the form is designed to be completed on a typewriter. In such cases, by all means *design* it on a typewriter. Too many times the spaces simply don't match, or there isn't enough room to contain the information required. Fill a sample in yourself as a test case. If you're tempted to slough it off, just think about how many hours have been wasted in trying to fit required information into the limited spaces of some of the more widely used and well-known government forms. I'm sure the reason more government workers don't change jobs is that the mere thought of doing a fresh SF171 is enough to give them conniption fits.

● legalisms

We devoted several pages to this subject in the chapter on how to write regulations. Let's single out a few here that deserve special mention. Weed them out every chance you get: *herein; hereinabove; therein; infra;* and *supra.* Doubtless you can add unfavorites of your own.

● less/fewer

This word pair gives many persons trouble. Careful writers recognize a well-defined difference between *fewer* and *less.* Use *fewer* in cases involving items, persons, etc., that can be counted; use *less* when you refer to matters of quantity or degree. For example, you should write "There are no *fewer* than 50 students in the class." BUT — "John has *less* capacity for learning than any of the other students."

● media/medium

I shouldn't have to remind you, but many writers constantly mix up *media* — which is plural — with *medium* — singular. Say *"The news media are . . ."* not *"The news media is . . . "*

● Murphy's law

Because I have spent a lot of time with scientists and engineers, I have mistakenly thought that everybody knows about Murphy's Law. Several of my readers have told me I am mistaken. That in itself is in a way a demonstration of Murphy's Law, as every engineer knows. For the rest of you, here is the way it goes:

1. Nothing is ever as easy as it looks.
2. Everything will take longer than you think it will.
3. If anything can possibly go wrong, it will.

The third item is the one that is usually quoted, but all three are equally valid and equally troublesome. If you like, you can add Aswell's Adjunct as number four on the list: Even if nothing can possibly go wrong, something will.

● noun clusters (also known as "noun adjuncts")

Administrative writing abounds with *noun clusters.* These are groups of nouns piled end to end; some of them may be used as *nouns,* others as *adjectives,* and perhaps still others in oddball permutations and combinations. Careful writers avoid these confusing constructions by using a sprinkling of prepositional phrases. Don't write, for example, *the new car regulation,* or *the expired certificate renewal.* This kind of writing confuses the reader, who must try to figure out whether you are talking about a new car or a new regulation; an expired certificate or an expired renewal.

Here is one of the best (read *worst*) examples of noun clusters that I've encountered lately. It's the sign on the door of a Montgomery County (Maryland) office:

ROCKVILLE CORRIDOR TRANSPORTATION IMPROVEMENT
ALTERNATIVES FEASIBILITY STUDY PROJECT OFFICE

● numerals

According to the *GPO Style Manual*, "Most rules for the use of numerals are based on the general principle that the reader comprehends numerals more readily than numerical word expressions, particularly in technical, scientific, or statistical matter." GPO also says that "Arabic numerals are generally preferable to Roman numerals."

Some of the rules are quite complicated. If you are in doubt, by all means check with the *GPO Manual,* if you work for the government, or with the *University of Chicago Style Manual,* if you work for private industry.

Here are a few rough rules of thumb that will get you by most of the time:

- Spell out numbers of ten and below: one, two, three, etc.
- Use figures for numbers of 11 and higher.
- If you have combinations of numbers above and below ten in a single sentence, be guided by the one that comes first, and make the rest consistent. For example, *Each of 15 major commodities (9 metal and 6 nonmetal) was in short supply.* BUT *Although only nine major commodities were in short supply, restrictions were placed on thirteen more.*
- Don't begin a sentence with numerals. Spell out — for example, *Twenty-one persons attended.* Many times you can rephrase the sentence so that it doesn't start with the number. Instead of saying *One hundred persons or more failed the test,* say *More than 100 persons failed the test.*

● organization — methods of

cause and effect — This is the name of a standard method of development or organization. It is designed to stress the connection between a result and a preceding event. Use it to explain why something happened, or why you predict something is going to happen.

chronological order —Writing things down in the order they occur in "real time" is usually a good way to help the reader under stand. Most people's minds seem to be geared to chronological order; they naturally think that way. By going along with this built-in "instinct," you can often avoid many problems.

sequential method — This "step-by-step" method lends itself naturally to certain types of material, such as explaining a process, or describing a mechanism in operation. It is also the best and most logical method for writing *instructions.*

The main advantage of the sequential method of development is that it's easy to follow because the steps lock right in with the elements of the process or the operation being described.

● organization — a checklist for

1. Think before you write.
2. State your purpose and stick to it.
3. Get straight to the point; catch and hold the reader's attention.
4. Answer the questions Who-What-Where-When-Why-How, not necessarily in that order.
5. Move from the known to the unknown; from the simple to the complex; from the general to the specific.
6. Arrange your material so that one step clearly leads to the next.
7. Pay close attention to format — headings, paragraphing, etc. Give the reader as many "handles" on the material as you possibly can.
8. Use good transitions that clearly show relationships.
9. Keep time sequences in your writing in actual chronological order whenever possible.
10. Sum up! Remind your readers of the important items you want them to remember.

● overpunctuation

If you find you're having to use too many commas and parentheses to keep your ideas sorted out, chances are you'd better take a fresh look. Check your sentence constructions and word orders.

Beware of meandering off on side trails, however interesting they may seem at first glance. If you don't stick to the subject, you greatly increase the chances of losing your readers. (I often wish I could follow this advice myself.)

● please, thank you, and other amenities

Many high officials of government and industry are so accustomed to giving orders that they tend to forget the amenities. Ex-military officers perhaps have some excuse. The services aren't much for saying "please." But even ex-officers can be reminded, very politely, that a few "pleases" and "thank yous" won't hurt a thing.

When you are editing, pay special attention in changing passives to actives. Instead of changing "The report will be submitted" to "Submit the report," how's about trying *"Please* submit the report." The imperative remains imperative, and you're much more likely to accomplish the desired objective.

● precipitant/precipitous

These words are often confused. *Precipitant* is an adjective that means "falling steeply or headlong." (*Precipitate* means essentially the same thing, but can be either a noun or an adjective.) *Precipitous* is an adjective meaning "steep." Thus, you should write that a person made a *precipitant* decision, NOT a *precipitous decision.*

● precision in writing — checklist for

Here's a checklist to help make your writing more precise:

1. Know your audience. Find out as much as you can about your readers, and what they already know, before you write.
2. Aim directly, with a specific purpose, at a central subject.
3. Use exact words. Look them up if you're not sure.
4. Use nouns and verbs that are meaningful to the senses— particularly sight, hearing, and touch.
5. Quantify. Give exact figures when you can, not imprecise generalities.
6. Be as careful with punctuation as you are with words.
7. Check all the facts. Then double check. Use original sources whenever you possibly can.
8. Avoid ambiguity. Be especially watchful for *squinting constructions, improper noun references,* and *dangling constructions.*
9. Omit all extraneous material.
10. Point up the important aspects of the subject. Don't make your readers do detective work.

● predicate (see under sentence — the parts of)

● preposition — ending a sentence with

Somewhere along the way you have probably been cautioned never to end a sentence with a preposition. Nonsense. As some wag once said, "A preposition is often an excellent word to end a sentence with."

There is an even more famous quotation on the subject. This one is ascribed to Winston Churchill. The story goes that an editor "corrected" one of the great man's manuscripts by marking up a sentence that ended with a preposition. The indignant Winnie responded, "This is the kind of arrant pedantry, up with which I shall not put."

● proofreading

We all know that in manuscript a minor error can slip by even a very careful proofreader. Why is it? As soon as a mistake appears in cold black type, it seems to be instantly visible to everyone who reads it. And all those readers will take fiendish delight in calling or writing to raise hell.

There is a famous case, perhaps apocryphal, of a 19th Century British publisher who decided to produce the most beautiful book in the history of printing. He signed up the best artists, the best craftsmen, the best printers, the best everything he could find. He spared no expense to ensure perfection. Years went by, as every step was checked and rechecked. But, or so the story goes, when the book finally came off the press, it had a typographical error in the title — in 40-point type. Murphy's Law may not have been formulated at that time, but its truth was certainly demonstrated.

Take heed, dear reader. It's not enough to proofread your own copy. You may detect some of the mistakes, but you will certainly miss others. All writers are more or less blind to their own copy because they are too familiar with it. It looks to them the way they think it is *supposed* to look.

That's why professionals know that proofreading must be done in pairs — with one person holding the original copy while the other reads the final version aloud.

Good proofreaders are hard to find, but with practice on your own copy and that of others, you can sharpen your editorial eye. Work both sides of the street. Sometimes you can be the "copyholder" who reads aloud to the proofreader, noting every paragraph indention, all capital letters and punctuation marks, and any special instructions to the printer that are indicated on the copy. You can even sound as if you know what you are doing by using the special short forms that professional copyreaders use:Say "pos" for "apostrophe," "bold" for "boldface," "cap" for "capital," "cap and low" for "capitals and lower case," "com" for "comma," "three points" for "ellipsis," "bang" for "exclamation point," "hife" for "hyphen," "ital" for "italic," "pare" or "graf" for "paragraph," "paren, close paren" for "parenthesis," "point" for "period," "query" for "question mark," "quote, close quote" for "quotation marks," and "sem" for "semi-colon."

The copyreader must be sure to pronounce every word clearly. Read slowly enough that the proofreader will have time to make any changes or corrections or queries on the galley or page proof.

Don't slough off this important task. The mistakes you prevent may be your own.

NOTE: Even after you have corrected galleys, don't trust the typesetter to correct them properly; look out for other errors made in the process. Always proof "corrected" proofs!

● punctuation — the importance of

Many writer's handbooks begin with a discussion of *punctuation* — the system of symbols used by writers to help readers understand structural relationships of elements within a sentence. Because so many truly excellent books *are* available, I have chosen to be skimpy on this subject — particularly since it is far too important to be treated properly in a short space.

Most authorities recognize two "schools" of punctuation: *open* and *closed*. Observation leads me to believe that most members of my generation prefer the *closed* system, which employs far more marks (primarily commas) than does the *open* system espoused by most young people — particularly those in the newspaper business.

Frankly, my elderly colleagues and I are in the minority. Most writers nowadays follow newspaper practice — the fewer punctuation marks, the better.

I'll do my best to stay out of the conflict. Instead, I'll recommend two respected authorities. If you work for private industry, get a copy of *The University of Chicago Style Manual*. If you work for the government, use the *GPO Style Manual*. (I disagree violently with much of it, but I have never yet won a single argument where it was invoked as the authority!)

Another good (and inexpensive) reference is *Punctuate It Right*, by Harry Shaw (Barnes and Noble). Shaw is stricter than many other modern authorities. That's probably why I like him so well. His book explains not only what punctuation marks to use, but *why* Shaw believes you should use them.

The approach is thorough, covering more aspects of punctuation than you'd ordinarily find. Shaw goes into separate discussions for each mark, and gives a glossary of terms often used in grammar. He also furnishes an excellent section on applied punctuation.

So as not to cop out entirely, I've given you a few rules of thumb under appropriate headings, including *commas, hyphens,* and *quotation marks.* These entries will solve the more common problems. If they aren't enough, refer to the experts.

● quotation marks

Here are a few rules of thumb on quotation marks. First, however, let's bear in mind that there are several widely differing schools of thought on this subject. British practice, in particular, differs quite markedly from what we are setting forth here. My "authority" for this particular approach is the well-known columnist of the *Washington Post,* Bill Gold. He is a man deeply concerned about language, and I have learned much from his wise and witty comments over the years.

Bill Gold suggests that working writers paste the following rules on their typewriters:

1. Commas and periods always go *inside* quotation marks.

2. Colons and semicolons always go *outside.*

3. The interrogation point and exclamation point go *inside* quotation marks *only* when they are part of the quotation. Otherwise they go *outside.*

EXAMPLES:

"He said, 'Would you like to do as you please?' "
"Does it make sense to tell him, 'Do as you please'?"
He said, "If you do it your way, I'll kill you!"
"Instead of telling me how to handle the crisis, he said, 'Do as you please' "!

— "The District Line," (*Washington Post,* November 8, 1976.)

● quotations — importance of getting them right

When you use quotations in your writing, take special care to make them accurate. Go to the original source if possible; secondary sources can, and often will, mislead you. Many famous quotations are really famous *mis*quotations. For example, does "Water, water everywhere, and not a drop to drink," sound right to you? It isn't.

How about "blood, sweat, and tears"? Wrong again. Actually, what Winston Churchill said when he took office as Prime Minister was "blood, toil, tears, and sweat." These examples are from an insufferably scholarly book called *The Dictionary of Misinformation,* by Tom Burnham (Ballantine Books). The book is infuriating, because it demonstrates that "so much of what most of us know ain't so." (That, incidentally, is a misquotation from Josh Billings.)

In writing this book I ran across a few problems with quotations. For example, I wanted to use Winston Churchill's famous remark about ending sentences with prepositions. The quotation is well known and widely used, but it has never been fully documented, at least so far as I have been able to find. One book of quotations says, "This is the sort of thing up with which I shall not put." It doesn't ring true. I can't believe that Winnie, so precise about language, would have used an imprecise and sloppy word such as "thing" in that context.

Another book says, "This is the sort of nonsense up with which I will not put." That sounds closer, but still doesn't ring the bell.

I finally remembered that the first time I ever encountered the quotation was in Rudolph Flesch's excellent book, *The Art of Readable Writing* (p. 149). I looked it up again there, and found the version I believe to be correct: — "This is the kind of arrant pedantry, up with which I shall not put." Thank you, Rudolph Flesch. I can't prove a thing, but in my heart I know you're right. (Although I'd quibble about the comma.)

Another problem was my Latin quotation from Caesar's *Gallic Wars.* My hazy recollection from schoolboy days was that the opening passage ran, "Omnis Gallia in tres partes divisa est." Several friends warned me that my recollection was incorrect. One referred me to *Bartlett's,* which reads, "Gallia est omnis divisa in tres partes."

I didn't have the gall (sorry about that) to argue with Bartlett, but that didn't sound right to me. I found an interlinear translation — a "pony" — in a secondhand bookstore. The pony reads, "Omnis Gallia est divisa in tres partes." Unfortunately, as I later discovered, the pony rearranged some sentences to make them easier to translate into English. When I finally took the Metro down to Washington's fine Martin Luther King Library and dug out Caesar's work in the original Latin, I found that Bartlett was right. What a lot of bother when the point I was using the quotation to prove was that the Romans could say things in more than one way!

Writing speeches for the space program some years ago, Jim Aswell ran across a Victor Hugo quotation: "Nothing is stronger than an idea whose time has come." It's a lovely quote, but Hugo didn't say it, or at least not in those words. Research disclosed that the original French was something about "Stronger than the tread of mighty armies is an idea whose time has come."

One last example. Back in the early '60s, Jim Aswell wrote a stirring speech for NASA Administrator James E. Webb. Jim made up a cute little anecdote with the punchline "When it's steamboat time, you steam." To give the story an aura of respectability and, as Jim put it, verisimilitude, he ascribed the story to Mark Twain.

Mr. Webb's speech went over big. It was quoted widely in newspapers across the country. I'm told that Mark Twain scholars have been looking for the original "steamboat" quote ever since. They are not likely to find it. (I hope they read this book and call off the search.)

● readability formulas

Rudolph Flesch, Robert Gunning, Edgar Dale, John McElroy. Do these names sound at least vaguely familiar to you? If not, it's time you were introduced. These are among the best known of the many writers, psychologists, linguists, and other scholars who have turned their attention to the many problems of making writing more "readable." (There is a difference between "readable" and "effective," although the two usually go together.)

For a long time I thought that Flesch was the pioneer in this field. Later, I learned that he had many predecessors; he was, however, the first to popularize the subject of readability: first with his book *The Art of Plain Talk* (1946), then with *The Art of Readable Writing (1949).* I commend them both to you. Flesch, unlike some others in the field, is quite good at practicing what he preaches.

Robert Gunning is another real "pro," perhaps even more widely known than Rudolph Flesch. Gunning's approach to measuring readability — called the "Fog Index" — has been widely used by both government and industry in recent years. In truth, Gunning's "Fog Index" and Flesch's "Readability Scale" are not all that different. Both are concerned primarily with two factors: (1) the average length of sentences, and (b) the percent of "difficult" words — that is, words having three or more syllables.

To use the Flesch system, one must employ a chart or — a less well-known but more accurate word — a *nomograph*. By making a couple of simple counts involving average sentence length and number of syllables per hundred words, you can easily come up with a "reading ease" score. You simply place a ruler or straight-edge on the appropriate numbers on the two outside columns of his nomograph, and observe where they cross a center line labeled the "Reading Ease" score. That score can range from zero (for extremely difficult material) to 100 (for very easy material).

Because I am really terrible at arithmetic, I like the Flesch formula, which requires little effort on my part. The trouble is, you must have the nomograph on hand. And, of course, many times when you need it you simply won't have it available.

Doubtless that explains why Gunning's "Fog Index" has achieved somewhat wider usage. It is easy to commit the formula to memory, and then you can work out a score any time, anywhere. (If you're good at math!)

As I mentioned earlier, the basic ingredients are essentially the same in these two well-known methods. (Indeed, so far as I know, they — sentence lengths and syllable counts — are key elements in any of the other going methods designed to quantify readability.) With both Flesch and Gunning methods, your first step is to pick a 100-word sample and figure the average sentence length. Next, you count the number of "difficult" words (that is, words having three syllables or more) in the sample. You then add the average number of words per sentence to the number of "difficult" words per hundred. Then, in the Gunning version, you multiply the result by 0.4. The result, rounded off to the nearest whole number, gives you the "Fog Index," which Gunning has cleverly designed to be roughly equivalent to the grade level a reader must have completed in order to understand the material. (The Fog Index of that last sentence would be appalling — but remember, you don't go on the basis of single sentences. You go by the *average*. And that is why I now hasten to throw in some short sentences.)

If all this does not seem clear, perhaps an example will help: Suppose that you find the average length of sentence is 15 words. Then you determine that the percentage of "difficult" words is 13. Add the 15 and the 13, and you come up with 28. Multiply the 28 by 0.4, and you get a Fog Index of 11.2, which you round off to 11 even. That means a person with an 11th grade education should be able to understand the material. (A score of 6 would mean a 6th grader could handle it. And so on.)

what readability formulas can and can't do

Nobody can learn to be a writer by using a mathematical formula. Indeed, I have seen many would-be writers mess themselves up by trying to apply the formula while they were actually writing. The result was horrendous. They would lose their flow of words, forget their thought patterns, and end up with nothing worth saving.

The formulas work just fine *after the fact,* but not *before* or *during.* Get the first draft down as fast as possible; don't worry in the least about long sentences and difficult words. You have time enough, when the draft is finished, to check with the formula. Then you can edit, re-write, or whatever else you need to do to bring the score within a desirable range.

Also remember this. A piece of writing with a bad score is almost undoubtedly unclear, unless the writer was or is a true master of the language. (Henry James, for example, is much admired by many for his extremely long and convoluted — but grammatically sound — sentences. Bully for him. I hate to make this dreadful confession, but I use old Henry's writing to cure my insomnia.)

On the other hand, a good score on the formula does not necessarily guarantee that writing is either good or clear. The formula cannot evaluate the content or information of a message; also, it cannot evaluate the style.

With these provisos in mind, I believe you can use readability scores to excellent advantage, *after the fact,* as I have said earlier. If you are arguing with a colleague about the readability of a particular item, when all else fails, trot out the formula. You may snatch victory from the jaws of defeat. Of course, if you try this on your boss, the converse could well be true.

the famous simple-minded Bates formula

Perhaps some of you readers are almost as bad at math as I am. If you panic at the thought of doing the arithmetic required to work out the Fog Index, I have a nice surprise for you.

We nonmathematicians need a quick-and-dirty system to tell when our sentences are getting too foggy. I won't vouch for the accuracy of the math, but here is the simple-minded system I've been using on my own prose for the last 25 years. Maybe that explains why it remains as foggy as it is.

Rudolph Flesch's famous nomograph tells us that "standard" reading ease (a numerical score of 60 to 70) could theoretically be achieved with an average sentence length of 30 words. To do this, however, you would have to use almost nothing but one-syllable words, and that's not too easy.

To get the desired score with much less trouble, the trick is to cut down to an *average* sentence length of about 20 words. That way, you can use more long words.

Now let's bring Robert Gunning's Fog Index into the computations. We'll assume a Fog Index of 12 is about equivalent to Flesch's "standard" reading ease. You can obtain this index by averaging 20 words per sentence with, say, about 10 percent "long" words — three syllables or more.

Actually, a Fog Index of 12 may be too high these days, since reading skills have been deteriorating sharply for more than a decade. A Fog Index of 10 would probably be a better goal to shoot for.

Well, here's my simple-minded formula. Any time you can knock two words out of a sentence, you'll reduce the fog index by roughly one point. OR, if you can shorten two "long" words, you'll get the same effect. If you can eliminate two *long* words, you'll bring that score down by two whole points — a consummation devoutly to be wished.

So, first of all, keep that average sentence length at 20 or under — if possible, well under. Then, if you find you have sentences that are too long, counterbalance them with some sentences that are very short. And, if that doesn't do the trick, go through cutting out excess verbiage until the score comes down.

●reduce/lessen

This word pair is confusing to many writers. All you need to remember is that *reduce* refers to a decrease in bulk; *lessen* refers to a decrease in number. Thus, you *reduce* your weight, but *lessen* the number of pounds showing on the scale.

●reference materials — guides to

There are several excellent one-shot books that tell you where to look up facts on many different subjects. One good one is the *New York Times Guide to Reference Material,* by Mona McCormack. This book has sections on newspapers and magazines, encyclopedias, books and literature, dictionaries, almanacs, atlases, history, poetry, politics, government, current events, science, speeches, sports, and many other items. It's really a who-what-where-when-how-why, etc. made easy. It's useful not because it gives you the needed information directly, but rather because it tells you *where* to look. And that is really the key to knowledge.

●relative pronouns — that/which/who

Much confusion exists concerning the proper usage of these three relative pronouns. It isn't any wonder. Many grammars are quite vague on the subject, or don't bring it up at all. And many topflight writers do not observe the distinctions.

In that case, why bother?

Simply because the distinctions can be extremely useful if you're concerned with making your writing more precise. And that's what this book is all about.

The principles involved are really simple and easy to master. Hark back to your schooldays. Remember what your English teacher told you about *restrictive* and *nonrestrictive* phrases and clauses? If you don't, you can refer to the discussion of *restrictive and nonrestrictive* on page 180 of this handbook. Perhaps I had better also remind you that the terms *essential* and *nonessential,* or *limiting* and *nonlimiting* can be used interchangeably.

Let's begin with the pronoun *that.* It's the easiest, and accordingly, the least misused. *That* is employed to introduce a statement that is *essential* to the meaning of a sentence. If the phrase or clause it introduces were left out, the sentence would become meaningless. *That* may refer to persons, animals, things, or ideas.

Which introduces statements that merely describe or explain; accordingly, these statements are *not essential* to the meaning. *Which* refers only to animals, things, or ideas. It is not used to refer to persons.

Who (like *which*) introduces statements that merely describe or explain; again, statements that are not *essential* to the meaning of the sentence. *Who* refers only to persons — not to animals, things, or ideas.

Now let's look at some examples:

Example One: essential to the meaning.

My car was the only one *that* wasn't wrecked in the accident.

(Obviously, the sentence would have no meaning at all if it read "My car was the only one in the accident." Therefore *that was not wrecked* is essential to the meaning.)

Example Two: not essential to the meaning.

My car was not wrecked, *which* is fortunate.

("My car was not wrecked" is a complete and understandable sentence. The rest of the statement, "which is fortunate," is not essential to the meaning — it merely adds a nonessential expression of gratitude that my car wasn't wrecked.)

Example Three: not essential to the meaning.

My father, *who* is a former college professor, is retired.

(The essential fact is contained in the statement "My father is retired." The explanation "who is a former college professor" is nonessential. On the other hand, if I had written "My father, who is a former college professor, is the one member of our family *that* enjoys smoking," the contrast should be clear This version plainly calls for *that* instead of who, for without the essential "that enjoys smoking," the sentence would lose its meaning.)

● research — getting to the bottom of things

Be curious — and suspicious. Don't take *anything* on faith. Mazie Worcester, one of the best technical editors I know, used to remind me, "Don't believe a word they say until they prove it. Add up all the numbers. Check out *all* the facts."

Also, if you run across a technical term and you're not sure exactly what it means, find out — even though the word may be a standard part of the vocabulary of the subject under discussion.

Experience shows— although it seems strange if not impossible — that a good editor can improve the writing in an abstruse scientific or technical report *without comprehending all the information it contains.* BUT, to do this, the editor must check closely with an expert at every stage and all along the line. Here's a reminder to paste on your typewriter. Look at it often:

> *One of the worst crimes an editor can commit*
> *is to introduce errors of fact into a report under the guise*
> *of making it easier to read and understand.*

Finally, none of this gives you an excuse NOT to understand the material, if all that stands in your way is the need for doing a bit of homework. Any report will be much improved if the editor doesn't cop out and give in to sloth. Even if you are not technically trained in the field, you might try Lil Abner's system: "Any fool kin unnerstan' this. *Ah* unnerstan's it."

● research methods (see bibliography cards, note cards, files)

● restrictive and nonrestrictive

You probably learned these terms in school. Or instead, you may have been taught *essential* and *nonessential,* or *limiting* and *nonlimiting.* No matter — they all mean the same thing.

A *restrictive* phrase or clause limits, or restricts, the meaning of what it modifies. If you take it out of the sentence, the essential meaning of that sentence will be changed or destroyed. Here's a simple punctuation rule to remember: *a restrictive* construction is NEVER set off by commas.

Examples: "All members *desiring to attend the game* should be at the bus stop before noon." (*desiring to attend the game* is restrictive.) "The dog *that barked all night* belongs to my neighbor." (*that barked all night* is restrictive.)

A *nonrestrictive* phrase or clause gives additional information about what it modifies, but you can get along without that information. It does not limit or restrict the meaning of the sentence. In effect, it's a parenthetical element. Your punctuation rule this time is this: *ALWAYS set off nonrestrictive elements with commas — one comma at the beginning, the other at the end.*

Examples: "The book, *which was on the bestseller list for months,* was banned in Boston."

"The instrument, *called a thermometer,* is used to measure temperature." (The italicized phrases in both sentences are nonrestrictive.)

● sentence — the parts of

subject — When we make a statement or ask a question, there is some word that indicates the person or thing we are talking or asking about. Thus, in the sentences *The airplane flies* and *The book is thick,* we say something about the *airplane* and the *book.* In the question *When did the mail arrive?* we ask something about the *mail.* A word that is used this way in a sentence is said to be the *subject* of the sentence. In the sentences given above, *airplane, book,* and *mail* are the subjects.

predicate — What we say or ask about the subject is called the *predicate.* In the sentences that have been given, *flies, is,* and *did arrive* are the predicates.

A noun or adjective that is joined to the subject by a form of *to be (is, are, was, were, will be, has been,* etc.) is called a *predicate noun (or predicate nominative)* or *predicate adjective.*

In the sentence *My father is a lawyer,* the word *lawyer* is a predicate noun. In the sentence, *Your cousin is sleepy,* the word *sleepy* is a predicate adjective.

direct object — Frequently the subject of a sentence is said to do something that directly affects a person or thing. In the sentence *The dog chased the rabbit,* the act that the subject does directly affects the rabbit. A word used to denote a person or thing directly affected by an act is said to be the *direct object.* In the sentence above, *rabbit* is the direct object. In like manner, in the sentences *My uncle climbed Mount Everest,* and *The flame burned the carpet,* the words *Mount Everest* and *carpet* are direct objects.

indirect object —An *indirect object* is a noun or pronoun used to denote the person to whom something is given, said, or shown.

● since/because

Many writers habitually use the word *since* as a synonym for *because*. Sometimes I do it myself, but that doesn't make it right. Remember that in its primary meaning, the word *since* denotes the passing of time. Use it to mean from then until now, or from some particular past time to the present. James J. Kilpatrick, a columnist who cares very much about language, recently wrote "When *since* is used in place of the honest *because,* the eye flickers and the mind stumbles." (*Washington Star,* July 6, 1976.)

● subject (see sentence — the parts of)

● sloppy constructions

"Language skills prevent our young people from performing their studies." No. *Lack of* language skills.

"Reduced speed ahead." (Sign frequently seen along Virginia highways.) No. *Reduce* speed ahead.

"This road only leads to higher prices." (sign in front of motel in Fairfax, Virginia.) No. This road leads *only* . . .

● talking down (or writing down)

This is a dreadful but prevalent sin. Like many other sins that are far more enjoyable, it can sneak up on any of us if we don't exercise constant vigilance. The best defense is to keep an imaginary reader constantly in mind — a bright and perceptive imaginary reader.

You certainly don't want to insult the intelligence of that paragon of readers, so you make an assumption — he or she may not know some of the facts you are explaining. That's probably why you are writing in the first place. But follow the golden rule of writing, and just tell your story. Your attitude alone can make all the difference.

● tantalizing/enticing

The advertising agencies have just about done us in on the distinction between these two words. *Tantalizing* is not by any means the same thing as *enticing*. To *tantalize* carries the connotation of torment or torture by arousing an intense desire for something that is forever withheld. Most of the time, *enticing* will be the word you want. If you don't like it, you might try *appetizing, provocative, savory,* or *tempting.* Remember that coffee does not have a "tantalizing" aroma unless you are forever denied the drinking of the glorious beverage.

● teaching machine logic

Dr. B. F. Skinner, in setting forth his gospel of programmed learning, said of the programmer: "His goal must be to keep refining his program until the point is reached at which the answers of the average child will almost always be right."

That's a good principle for writers to remember. Think about it the next time you try to explain a difficult or unfamiliar concept to your readers.

● title

The *title* of your writing enterprise is the first thing your reader sees. It is therefore the most important single *handle* to lead your reader to your project in the first place.

Accordingly, your title should perform at least these three important functions:

1. It should clearly indicate the specific subject or topic of the project.
2. It should suggest the project's scope and objectives.
3. It should grab the reader's attention.

Don't make your title too short or too vague. If you do, your reader may never be able to find your project or report in the first place, and all your work will have gone for nothing.

Put as many *key words* as possible in your title. That way, when your report is catalogued in publications guides, indexes, and computerized data systems, your reader will be able to track it down, even when coming at it from several different directions.

● transition

A *transition* is a guidepost or road sign for your readers. Sometimes the guidepost can be read in either direction — just as in the small town where I lived as a child. Opposite sides of the same sign read "Entering Warrenton," and "Leaving Warrenton."

The writer should strive to lead the reader as easily and painlessly as possible from one idea to the next. To do this is not really difficult, but it does require thoughtful attention.

Transition can be achieved by a word, a phrase, a sentence, or even a paragraph.

Certain words are particularly useful to show transition. Here are some suggestions:

To express addition, use *also, besides, furthermore, moreover, too.*

To express comparison, use *likewise* or *similarly.*

To express example, use *as an illustration, for example, for instance, specifically.*

To express result, say *as a result, consequently, hence,* or *therefore.*

Besides using transitional words and phrases such as those just listed, you can also achieve effective transition by (a) *repeating key words or phrases* from preceding sentences; (b) using *pronouns* that refer clearly to antecedents in previous sentences; and/or (c) using *parallel structure.*

● unnecessary repetition

As we have explained many times, a careful writer must always strive not to waste words — particularly by unnecessary repetition. Here's an example, out of a real document, that shows how NOT to write:

> It has been noted that not all persons who received training during the time frame have been noted. It has also been noted that the listing for some directorates reflect that none of its employees have received training.

● variety and style in writing

After you've mastered all the skills we've talked about up to now, and have practiced them until they become second nature, you're ready to start working on some of the refinements of the writing craft.

Of these, one of the most important is variety of sentence structure — the rhythms and cadences that, taken to the ultimate, will give you a recognizable writing style of your own.

Many professional writers will tell you the best way to acquire a good style is to study carefully the work of writers whose craft you respect. Read, and read some more. But learn to read critically, not simply for entertainment. If you happen to run across a piece of writing you think is particularly well done, try to figure out how the writer achieved the effects you admire.

In the "olden days," many writers — Robert Louis Stevenson is an example who comes immediately to mind — deliberately copied the works of the masters. In the process, writers learn not simply to imitate, but to create new effects of their own.

When I was growing up, every aspiring young jazz trumpet player wanted to play the way Louis Armstrong did. Roy Eldridge learned how to do that extremely well before he found out that he could play like Roy Eldridge. Later came Dizzy Gillespie, who could sound more like Eldridge than Eldridge himself, until Diz developed his own distinctive and revolutionary style.

MORAL: It's a good idea to learn the traditions and follow the rules set forth by the recognized craftsmen of the writing trade before you try too hard to do your own thing.

But, you might ask, are there any exercises an aspiring writer can practice, the way an ambitious young pianist might tackle Hanon and Czerny and the Bach two-part inventions?

Frankly, I don't know of very many. But here is a sampling of some simple "two-handed" studies you might try working on:

1. Make a conscious effort to vary the length of your sentences. If you tend toward long sentences, throw in some short ones — you might deliberately make them very short indeed, perhaps just a few words. Maybe just one. See? That not only varies the monotony, but also helps bring down your fog index.

2. Mix in a few periodic sentences. (DEFINITION: A *periodic sentence* is one in which the meaning of the main clause is not completed until the end of the sentence. It is the opposite of a *loose sentence,* which is one in which various details are added *after* the meaning of the main clause is complete. Short sentences are often periodic; long sentences tend to be loose.) A famous example of a periodic sentence comes to mind — a parody of the style affected in *Time* magazine during the years Henry Luce was in charge. The sentence went something like this: "Backward ran the sentences of *Time* until reeled the mind."

3. Strive to master the use of parallel construction. Study the beautifully balanced cadences of the Old Testament Psalms and the New Testament Beatitudes. Read — or better still, listen to — the "I Have A Dream" speech of the late Dr. Martin Luther King. Observe how he built that speech to greater and greater dramatic effects with every repetition, every cadence.

4. Experiment with sentence arrangements, particularly by altering the way you handle modifying phrases and parenthetical expressions. That is, try them at various locations within the sentence. Always make sure, of course, that you haven't created any ambiguities, or confused your readers with squinting constructions. (DEFINITION: *squinting constructions* —usually squinting modifiers — are words so placed in a sentence that they can be interpreted in two or more ways, according to whether they "look" at the words they precede or the words they follow.)

● voice — active and passive

The term *voice* is used in English grammar to indicate, by a change in the verb form, whether the subject *acts* (active voice) or is *acted upon* (passive voice).

Writers should strive to use the active voice whenever possible. By doing this, they will make their writing stronger, clearer, shorter, and more emphatic. For example:

ACTIVE: *I rang the bell. Theodore submitted the report. The cow jumped over the moon.*

PASSIVE: *The bell was rung by me. The report was submitted by Theodore. The moon was jumped over by the cow.*

As you can see, to form the passive versions, you take what was formerly the *direct object,* or *complement,* of the *transitive* verb and transform that word into the subject. You follow this by a verb phrase made up of some form of *to be* plus the *past participle.*

The passive voice is used far too much in most administrative writing. (If you are alert, you have noticed that I appear to have broken my own "rule" by using a passive here. You might well ask why I did not write, instead: "Most administrative writers use the passive far too much." After all, using the active version thus would be shorter. The active version is *always* shorter than the passive, without fail. It is also — *almost* always — stronger, more straightforward, and easier to understand.)

But, insofar as the point of my discussion is concerned, the passive version is preferable here. Does this confuse you? I don't blame you if it does. There are exceptions to almost every "rule," and this is a case in point. When you are writing about a particular subject at some length, as I am here, you logically should make the subject of your topic sentence the same as the subject of your essay. To start with "Most administrative writers" would put the emphasis in the wrong place. The paragraph is concerned primarily with the passive voice, not with administrative writers.

Another exception: when the doer of the action is unknown or unimportant, use the passive voice. Or if you deliberately want to be obscure, or to keep a low profile, or to avoid responsibility, by all means use the passive. You can't beat it!

●"-wise" as a suffix

The worlds of government and business seem to have gone wild about -*wise* as a suffix, as in *policy-wise.* Let's consign the whole kit and caboodle of them to Gehenna. Here's an illustration that should help convince you of the wisdom of this suggestion. I can't remember the source, but it purports to be a question asked of a wise old owl:

"Hey, owl, how are you doing wise-wise?"
The owl's answer: "Otherwise."

● writer's block

Just about everyone who's even faintly interested in writing has heard of "writer's block." Pray that you never suffer from it — the malady professional writers fear most.

Some writers I know are superstitious about it. They say one should never even mention the subject or even think about it. That attitude seems ostrich-like, to say the least. If you find you are being called upon to write more and more, take this advice: start forming the kinds of habits and attitudes most likely to protect you against having the well run dry.

The first important step you must take is to find out — assuming that you don't already know — what time of day you function best. Are you a morning person or a night person? My son Bill can't even get his motor running until the rest of us are ready to give up and go to bed. Some of his friends seem to be on the same schedule, so perhaps his pattern is not so unusual as I once thought. Unquestionably, differing biological rhythms among individuals mean that we can't expect all people to do their best work at the same time of day. By trial and error, you should be able to get your best time zeroed in.

Here, then, are a few tips:

1. Find out when your best creative time is, and try never to undertake any really demanding writing jobs except during your good hours. (It's hard enough to get started at best; we need to have everything going for us that we can manage.)

2. Set a regular pattern and routine. (Sometimes this can be carried to ridiculous lengths, or so it would appear. But don't knock it.)

3. [I am going to make you wait for this one. Have to tell you a couple of anecdotes first.]

A very famous writer of western stories, Zane Grey, was popular during my youth. Somewhere I've read that when he was getting started as a writer, he worked in a beat-up old morris chair. It was so delapidated that the stuffing was coming out, but it was all he could afford. Using an old board that he had cut to fit across the chair arms, he'd park his old Remington portable there, lean back in his chair, and blaze away.

The system worked. He became successful and the money started to roll in. Then his wife, as wives will, decided to surprise him on his birthday. She donated his chair and typewriter to the Salvation Army, and bought him a fancy new chair and a fancy new typewriter. There was just one problem: poor old Zane could no longer write a word. He just couldn't get cranked up to write under those posh but unfamiliar conditions. He had to rush down to the Salvation Army and buy back his old chair and typewriter. (I understand they threw in the board at no extra charge.) The whole story may or may not be true, but if it isn't, it ought to be. It has the ring of verisimilitude. (That's a nice long word that seems appropriate in this context, so to hell with the rule about preferring simple words.)

Another good example of a writer with bizarre habits is Thomas Wolfe, the late novelist from North Carolina, not to be confused with the living journalist Tom Wolfe. Thomas Wolfe was about six foot six, and he wasn't at all comfortable sitting at desks designed for persons of average size. He discovered he could write best standing up, using the top of a refrigerator for a desk. It was just the right height. Whenever he ran out of ideas he'd pace up and down the kitchen and then come back and write some more. He was so enormously productive that sometimes he'd write for up to 16 or 18 hours at a stretch when things were going well.

I understand that Wolfe never had trouble with writer's block except once or twice when he was in Europe and couldn't find a refrigerator the right height. Apocryphal? Probably not.

Another "stand-up" writer was the man who may have been the greatest master of the English language since James Joyce. I refer to Vladimir Nabokov, who died recently. (What is most depressing to me is that English was Nabokov's *second* language. He is reputed to have written even better in Russian.) Nabokov always wrote standing up, and he always did his initial drafts on index cards. We can wonder what happened if he ran out of cards.

The famous German poet, Schiller, had some kind of Freudian quirk whose significance I don't pretend to understand. Apparently he wrote most creatively only when he had a basket of half-rotten apples on his desk. The smell apparently stimulated his imagination. Don't ask me why.

Here's one final tip. Many professional writers use it and say it works for them. Maybe it will work for you as well.

> 3. When you get to the end of your day's production, stop right in the middle of a sentence that is going well.

The psychology is this: When you return to work the next day, you can start getting up speed by finishing that unfinished sentence. The rest of the sentence should come easily, and with luck, will stimulate you to continue.

I leave you with this good advice, and with the heartfelt hope that writer's block will never happen to you. Although you are not yet a "professional" writer in the sense that you are writing for a living, if you have studied this book well you can at least approach your writing tasks in a professional way.   "May the force be with you," as the *Star Wars* fans are saying these days, or — in the language of the "olden days," — Hail and farewell!

PART THREE

ADDITIONAL EXERCISES

by

Louis J. Hampton

CHARLES E. WATERMAN, executive vice-president of Speak/Write Systems, Inc., shares with the author of this book some of the teaching and consulting work of the company. His classes in effective writing for universities, major corporations, and government have been presented coast to coast in the United States and into Canada.

An experienced public speaker and a former professional speechwriter, he is the prime instructor and speech coach for Speak/Write in all of the company's oral communication programs. He has received numerous awards both for his speaking abilities and for his management skills.

Other experience includes service as a city-beat reporter on a daily newspaper, and film direction and screenwriting with assignments that took him to every corner of the nation and to England, Germany, and Japan. Later he headed a technical editing program with a staff of editors, graphic artists, and layout technicians.

He has taught at a number of major universities, including The American University, Georgetown, and George Washington, in addition to his regular teaching duties for Speak/Write. He frequently serves as a book editor, and has aided many published writers to put their manuscripts into acceptable final form for the printer.

LOU HAMPTON is president of his own firm, Hampton Communication Strategies. Formerly associated with Speak/Write's predecessor firm, he wrote a number of exercises for earlier editions of this book. Some of these have been carried over to the current edition.

EXERCISE ONE. Passive Constructions

Rewrite the following sentences, changing passives to actives whenever you believe the change is appropriate. You may keep the passive construction if you can explain why you consider it preferable.

1. It has been pointed out that American influence abroad is weakened by dissent at home.
2. It was suggested that the construction schedules be revised by the project manager.
3. Compilation of the finance data should be completed by branch managers no later than July 1st.
4. Room reservations should be scheduled by the attendees.
5. Local issues, it was reported by newsmen, are the causes for the strike.
6. Daniel J. McGower was named vice president, manufacturing and development, for the Hamilton, Ontario, branch of IBM.
7. It was decided by the commissioner that more decisions should be made by the regional offices.
8. A reduction in job-related accidents was achieved by an incentive program.
9. Delivery of all items must be achieved by the carrier within five work days.
10. The regulations specify that research must be conducted by technically qualified personnel.
11. Permission must be received from the commanding officer before new projects may be started.
12. Under the new policy, sales goals will be established by the national office.
13. A progress report should be submitted weekly.
14. It is expected that this basic plan will be supported by the salespersons as well as the salesmanagers.
15. Feedback would be hampered by the complicated forms.

EXERCISE TWO. Smothered Verbs

Get rid of the smothered verbs in the following sentences. Make any other editorial changes you believe will improve clarity.

1. To effect a proper utilization of time, ensure that preparation of an agenda has been accomplished before the meeting.

2. Mr. Lynn will need reissuance of his credentials with a reflection of his new title.

3. The improvement in the return on portfolio is a result of an increase in the average yield on the mortgage portfolio.

4. The Nuclear Regulatory Commission was accused of a failure to force compliance on nuclear powered plants by the G.A.O.

5. There is little guarantee that the bill would lead to improvements in the agency's efficiency, accountability, and effectiveness.

6. Assessment of the situation should precede implementation of the program.

7. Although a significant reduction in the budget was achieved by the standardization of the reporting system, the business still succumbed to failure.

8. An announcement was made by the President that a revision would be made in the government's fast breeder reactor program.

9. Implementation of these guidelines should be accomplished immediately.

10. After your completion of the registration process, proceed directly to the Alexander Hamilton Room.

11. Individualization of learning programs should be a more frequent occurrence in the public schools.

12. The candidate sought the discreditation and defeat of his opponent.

13. Institutionalization of the patient cannot be achieved without the procurement of a court order.

14. The committee reached a decision after extensive deliberation.

15. Rejection of the applicant without specific cause may result in the institution of grievance proceedings by the applicant.

EXERCISE THREE. Conciseness

Delete the deadwood from the following sentences; make them as concise as possible without altering shades of meaning.

1. Almost without exception, policy papers should be written to provide alternatives, although there are exceptions to this.

2. This point is not included in the sample papers that go to make up the enclosure.

3. The purpose of this memo is to provide a reference for the staff of the formats of various papers which go forward to the Commission.

4. There is a particular need to centralize assigning the change numbers for the various guides. At times, several individuals may be working on assigning change numbers in the same guide at the same time and are not aware of the change numbers assigned to other revisions.

5. Enclosed is a copy of last year's annual report for the fiscal year 1976.

6. The new manuals will be available for sales agents at a cost of $4.89 per each copy.

7. You will receive payment faster if we mail your checks rather than waiting for your agent to pick them up, since mail in the District of Columbia is usually delivered on a next-day basis.

8. It is my opinion that the cooperation shown by the employees and the cooperation shown by management was responsible for last year's increase in sales.

9. I currently work as the administrative officer for IPX's midwestern division and I administer all of IPX's programs in that division.

10. At some point in time we must decide on whether or not we are going to build the new addition.

11. Will Rogers was a man who liked informality.

12. A strong economy will benefit each and every one of us.

13. We have received your deposit in the amount of $30.00 which we will hold pending receipt of the remaining $30.00.

14. Due to the fact that all the data was not available, we will withhold making a decision until such time as all the data is accessible.

15. The health care program offered by the company is a health care program which provides the greatest number of health benefits for an equivalent premium.

EXERCISE FOUR. Concrete vs. Abstract

Substitute concrete, specific terms for the more abstract and general ones. Use your imagination to change dull, vague statements into sentences that will build word pictures in the reader's mind.

1. The man moved painfully down the sidewalk without noticing things around him.

2. A college professor has set a government form to classical music, according to a report in a prominent newspaper.

3. Some people think one thing about the candidate, others something else.

4. The youth got into the car quickly and drove off rapidly.

*5. Build "ladders of abstraction" similar to the one described on page 45 of the text. Supply words in the blanks, with each term **above** another being more abstract, and each term **below** being more specific:*
Example:
BROADER TERM: *textbook*
MIDDLE TERM: *writer's guide*
NARROWER TERM: *"Writing With Precision"*
Now, try your hand at filling in the blanks:

BROADER TERM:	silverware	powered aircraft	mathematics
MIDDLE TERM:	.....	jet plane	.....
NARROWER:	soupspoon	.....	algebra
BROADER:	.....	.....	.....
MIDDLE:	.....	.....	.....
NARROW:	windowpane	apple tree	police car
BROADER:	entertainment	soldier	structure
MIDDLE:	.....	.....	.....
NARROW:	"Star Wars"	sergeant	bungalow

EXERCISE FIVE(A.) Misplaced Modifiers

Reorder the following sentences to place modifiers as close as possible to the words they are intended to modify.

1. The program provides additional services to participants running a wide gamut from transportation to advice.
2. The public affairs officer described satellite programs which are launched on boosters.
3. Based on a recent inspection of the plant, the safety director decided to revise the safety procedures.
4. Based on extensive testing, the physician recommended immediate surgery.
5. The new product was developed in two weeks that doubled the company's gross sales.
6. The announcer said, "I'll be back to tell you how to spend a month in Austria in a minute."
7. The director spoke to the intern with a harsh voice.

EXERCISE FIVE(B.) Dangling Modifiers

Edit these sentences to eliminate dangling modifiers.

1. Having been well coached by his campaign manager, the candidate's speech gathered support for the candidate.

2. Blinded by the approaching car's headlights, John's car swerved off the road into a ditch.

3. To learn the technique thoroughly, the first three exercises must be completed.

4. To receive full retirement benefits, the pension plan must be participated in for twenty years.

5. By reducing each situation to its simplest elements, the answer was discovered by the analyst.

6. Sitting at her desk, the secretary brought the mail to the director.

7. By substituting blue for black ink, the brochure gained greater visual impact.

8. After being rejected by three companies, my employment counselor suggested I rewrite my resume.

9. After researching the topic for five months, my supervisor cancelled the project. ·

10. By using less water for showers and washing, the water authority will be able to meet the demand for water throughout the summer.

11. While waiting for a client to return from lunch, the parking meter expired and a policeman ticketed my car.

12. To increase their sales, computers are being used by salesmen to place at least 12 additional telephone calls each hour.

13. After waiting six days for the jury to return a verdict, concern grew that the trial might end in a hung jury.

14. While on the floor, a page summoned the Senator to meet with a group of constituents.

15. While mowing the lawn, a new idea popped into the writer's head.

EXERCISE SIX. Unnecessary Shifts

Rewrite the following sentences to eliminate all unnecessary shifts.

1. In order for Sunshine Act procedures to be followed, include a statement in the Scheduling block.

2. I certainly appreciate the opportunity to have met with you and introduce you to our staff during your visit.

3. We have reviewed your draft and the following comments are submitted.

6. Mr. Cochran criticized the loan department and has even ask for a new loan officer.

7. Forest fires destroyed thousands of acres of timber as it roared through the valley.

8. The director believes it would be in the best interest of the manufacturer to report on the initial list all the chemicals they can.

9. Metro trains were delayed by a malfunctioning signal, causing many to be thirty to forty minutes late to work.

10. Although I was satisfied, the job seemed to require less imagination than expected.

11. Release the safety catch and the operator then turns the valve.

12. A frequent source of complaints were the difficulties encountered in registration.

13. Before starting your own business, you should decide how much money they require.

14. The possibility of additional federal regulations on airline operations cause concern among airline industry officials.

15. The best way to use the note pads is to check off cards as they become known and using the initials of the player showing the card is an additional aid.

EXERCISE SEVEN. The Simple Word

Rewrite these sentences, improving them by using simple words and phrases and making other changes that clarify their meaning.

1. Pursuant to the rules being promulgated as of this date by the publications division, endeavor to employ uncomplicated words in writing.

2. The maintenance of simplicity and the avoidance of circumlocution will enable your readers to achieve improved comprehension.

3. The expenditure for the purchase of this ballpoint pen was over five dollars.

4. As the customers languished in the checkout line, the functionaries at the register hold desultory rumor-monging sessions.

5. The turf, psychologically speaking, tends to have the appearance of being more verdant beyond the barrier prohibiting one's access thereto.

6. This problem completely flustrates me!

7. The occurrence of the accident took place on the circumvential highway that surrounds the city.

8. Textilewise, early repairs are estimated to be nine times more efficacious than when remedial measures are significantly delayed.

9. The author transported his typewriter to the repair emporium in order to accomplish the purpose of removing contamination from its internal components.

10. The lunar orb radiated a lustrous iridescence on the limpid surface of the lake.

EXERCISE EIGHT(A.) Unnecessary Repetition

Rewrite the following sentences to eliminate unnecessary repetition.

1. One of the clerk's responsibilities is the compiling of time and attendance reports. These time and attendance reports go to the branch chief, who verifies that the information on each time and attendance report is accurate and complete.

2. Next year's proposed budget needs to be revised before being released to the public. Otherwise the budget may draw sharp criticism, because it is not a zero-based budget.

3. Mr. Jensen received 21 excellent ratings, 5 good ratings, and no poor ratings.

4. The information obtained from the study should be reported to the committee by June 23. All information should be complete; any information that is not complete should be clearly marked "incomplete."

5. Although industry officials view the proposed regulations as unnecessary, they are less opposed to these regulations than to the regulations proposed last year.

EXERCISE EIGHT(B.) Elegant Variation

Rewrite the following paragraph to eliminate elegant variation.

Each owner of an automobile is required to register the car within 30 days of the time of the purchase of the vehicle. The driver must report the car's serial number, engine number, make, and model. The owner must also indicate whether the vehicle is used for business purposes. Finally. days of the time of the purchase of the vehicle. The driver must report the car's serial number, engine number, make, and model. The owner must also indicate whether the vehicle is used for business purposes. Finally, the owner must indicate whether he bought the automotive conveyance at a recognized automotive vehicle dealer's establishment. No unlicensed personal car will be permitted to operate.

EXERCISE NINE. Parallel Construction

Rewrite the following sentences, following the principle of parallel structure.

1. Save gasoline by avoiding jack-rabbit starts, maintaining an even speed, and look ahead to anticipate signal changes.

2. I would like to learn the following from this book:
    1) How to start writing,
    2) Punctuation,
    3) How to develop style.

3. See immediate returns from the course through greater filing efficiency, quicker insurance claims processing, and collecting overdue accounts.

4. Four methods of providing company training are
- three-day seminars
- correspondence courses
- hiring a consultant
- in-house sessions.

5. Please observe the following regulations:
- Equipment must be reserved two weeks ahead;
- Removing equipment without signing out is not approved;
- Equipment must be returned within 48 hours of use.

6. I have nothing to offer but blood, toil, crying, and sweating.

7. The manager described the department's problems succinctly, clearly, and with candor.

8. Reviewing the records daily is as important as to collect accurate information.

9. Charles Jarvis is an excellent lecturer, personable conversationalist, and he writes well also.

10. With malice toward none, having charity for all, firmness in the right, let us strive on to finish the work we are in, effect a binding up of the nation's wounds, caring for him who shall have borne the battle, to do all which may achieve and cherish a just and lasting peace among ourselves and with all nations.

EXERCISE TEN(A.) Orderly Arrangement

Rewrite the following memo, using a more logical arrangement. Don't forget to apply all the other principles you have learned.

In accordance with your instructions, which you transmitted to me telephonically during the prior week, a search of the literature has been made and the undersigned has arrived at the determination that any one of the following copying machines should be entirely satisfying in fulfilling the needs of your department.

The Whizbang Model OD-227 has a selling price of $1985. It has demonstrated the capability of making 20 copies per minute. The maximum size of paper it is capable of handling is fairly large—up to eleven inches in one dimension and seventeen in the other. It will make reasonably good, but not excellent, copies on both sides of a sheet, if you so desire that feature. A service contract can be arranged for $400 per annum.

The Tolable Model 3-D will make copies anywhere from postcard size up to legal size. It is very fast—40 copies a minute. It is probably the best machine in its price range for making two-sided copies. The service contract is $600 per year. Cost of the machine itself is $2495.

The Copycat Model 1347 is reported to have a demonstrated capability of making one copy every five seconds. It will make enlargements and reductions, and can handle copies up to double the size of a standard 8-½ by eleven inch page. It is not recommended for making copies on both sides of a sheet of paper. Its selling price is just $1995, and a service contract is only $275 for a period of 12 months.

EXERCISE TEN(B.) Orderly Arrangement — correct order

Here is a description, in the wrong order, of the easy way to outline. Rearrange the items in a more logical progression.

1. The idea should be easy to grasp with a quick glance.
2. Spread out the cards on a table.
3. Check each pile to be sure the ideas are related.
4. Use 3x5, 4x6, or 5x8 cards.
5. Make a topic card for each pile.
6. Write only one idea on each card.
7. Rearrange topic cards to try many sequences until you are satisfied with one particular sequence.

8. In writing down the idea, use as few words as possible.

9. Put related ideas together in piles.

10. Here is the procedure for organizing an easy outline.

11. Discard ideas that, on re-examination, do not seem to fit the topic.

12. With the cards in order, you have completed your "easy outline."

13. Write down on the top of the cards the ideas that must be included in the report.

14. Using abbreviations will help.

15. Decide on a sequence to present your ideas.

16. One idea per card allows flexibility of thought.

17. Study the cards carefully.

18. Make cards for new ideas that come to mind.

EXERCISE TEN(C.) Writing Instructions

The following information is given in steps, as any good instruction should be. But the steps as shown are not arranged in the proper order. Rearrange them for the best logic, so that the reader is led properly from one step to the next.

Step 1. Check to see that language and nomenclatures in the illustrations are consistent with those of the text.

Step 2. Present each step in its normal order.

Step 3. Divide the process into distinct steps.

Step 4. Go through all the steps to see if they're in the right order, if they tell the reader all necessary information, and if they really work.

Step 5. Write an opening paragraph to set the stage. Explain the purpose of the entire operation. Give the reader a clear view of what is expected. (Find out what the reader already knows before you start!)

Step 6. Rewrite, rewrite, rewrite, as many times as necessary to achieve clarity.

Step 7. Check for and eliminate uncommon words and complicated phrasing. Define technical terms if necessary.

Step 8. If necessary, divide the text with appropriate headings and subheadings.

Step 9. *Show* the reader. Use working drawings, charts, illustrations, schematics, etc.

ANSWERS TO EXERCISES

EXERCISE ONE. Passive Constructions — suggested answers

1. Dissent at home weakens American influence abroad.
2. It was suggested that the project manager revise the construction schedule.
3. Branch managers should compile finance data by July 1.
4. Attendees should make room reservations.
5. [Since local issues are probably more important in this sentence than the newsmen, leave the sentence in the passive.]
6. [Here again, the name of the person being appointed is more important than that of the one doing the appointing; leave in the passive.]
7. The commissioner decided that the regional offices should make more decisions.
8. An incentive program reduced job-related accidents.
9. The carrier must deliver all items within five work days.
10. The regulations specify that technically qualified personnel must conduct the research. [If you want extra emphasis on the personnel, leave the sentence in the passive.]
11. The commanding officer must approve new projects before they may be started. [Notice that the second part of the sentence remains in the passive since we don't know who would be starting the projects.]
12. Under the new policy the national office will establish sales goals.
13. Submit a progress report weekly.
14. Salespersons as well as sales managers will, we expect, support this basic plan.
15. Complicated forms would hamper feedback. [Many writers take a dim view of *feedback*. I think it's a useful word here.]

EXERCISE TWO. Smothered Verbs — suggested answers

1. To use time properly, prepare an agenda before the meeting. [Why not "utilize"? Isn't that the verb form of "utilization"? Yes, it is. But "use" is shorter and less stuffy.]
2. Mr. Lynn will need his credentials reissued to reflect his new title. [Or simply: " . . . with his new title."]
3. The return on portfolio improved because the average yield on the mortgage portfolio increased.
4. GAO accused the Nuclear Regulatory Commission of failing to force compliance on nuclear power plants. [Perhaps you put, " . . . to force nu-

clear powered plants to comply." That might be fine for most of us lay persons, but it would upset the regulators to whom *compliance* has a specific meaning. They have pages of regulations defining *compliance*. So be careful not to change words that have special connotations to specific groups of readers.]

5. There is little guarantee that the bill would improve the agency's efficiency, accountability, and effectiveness.

6. The situation should be assessed before the program is implemented. [Or more simply: "Look before you leap."]

7. Although the budget was significantly reduced by standardizing the reporting system, the business still failed.

8. The President announced that the government's fast breeder reactor program would be revised. [Note the appropriate use of the passive. Since we don't know who will revise the program, we must keep the second part of the sentence in the passive.]

9. Implement these guidelines immediately.

10. After you register, proceed [go] to the Alexander Hamilton Room.

11. Individualized learning programs should occur more frequently in the public schools. [Or better, "Public schools should fit more learning programs to the ability of the individual."]

12. The candidate sought to discredit and defeat his opponent.

13. The patient cannot be institutionalized without a court order. [Many editors would object to *institutionalize*. If we knew the specific institution, we could get rid of the word easily; for example, ". . . cannot be placed in a mental hospital," or ". . . in a detention home," etc. Even without knowing, many editors would probably change this to read ". . . cannot be placed in an institution. . ."]

14. After deliberating extensively, the committee decided.

15. An applicant rejected without specific cause may institute [begin] grievance proceedings.

EXERCISE THREE. Conciseness — suggested answers

1. Almost without exception, policy papers should provide alternatives.

2. This point is not included in the samples.

3. This memo gives examples of the formats for papers that go to the Commission.

4. There is a need to centralize assigning the change numbers for the

various guides. At times, several individuals may be working on assigning numbers in the same guide, unaware of numbers assigned to other revisions. [Or: "There is a need to centralize assigning the change numbers for the various guides to avoid duplication.]

5. Enclosed is the report for fiscal 1976. [*Copy* is an over-used word; it is rarely necessary in most writing. The difference between a Cezanne and a copy of a Cezanne is significant. The distinction between the annual report and a copy of the annual report is difficult to determine . . . and certainly not worth the effort.]

6. Sales agents may purchase the new manuals for $4.89 each.

7. You will receive payment faster if we mail your checks, since mail in the District of Columbia is usually delivered the next day. We now often wait four or five days for your agent to pick up the check.

8. I believe that the cooperation of management and employees was responsible for increasing sales last year.

9. I am the administrative officer for IPX's midwestern division and am responsible for all its programs.

10. Sometime we must decide whether to build the new addition.

11. Will Rogers liked informality.

12. A strong economy will benefit each of us.

13. We have received your $30.00 deposit which we will hold until we receive the remaining $30.00.

14. We will decide after receiving all the data.

15. The health care program offered by the company provides the greatest number of benefits for the price.

EXERCISE FOUR: Concrete vs. Abstract—suggested answers

1. The 90-year-old man limped down the crowded sidewalk with a glance at the squealing pre-schoolers playing hopscotch.

2. Edwin Avril, music professor at Glassboro State College, has set the 1040 tax form to the music of Bach's Easter Cantata, according to a report in the *Wall Street Journal.*

3. Young voters consider the Coalition's candidate, Betty Markham, to be perfect for the Silver Creek school board vacancy, while old-timers say they doubt she has the maturity to handle the teachers' demands for more authority in the classroom.

4. Jim, the star quarterback of the Silver Creek "Silver Streaks," hopped into the front seat of his roadster without even opening the door, and gunned the engine as he rocketed out of the driveway.

5. Here are a few suggestions. (Your "ladders" may be better!)
silverware/spoon/soupspoon
entertainment/movie/"Star Wars"
opening/window/windowpane

EXERCISE FIVE(A.) Misplaced Modifiers — suggested answers

1. The program furnishes participants with additional services, running a wide gamut from transportation to advice.
2. The public affairs officer described satellite programs that involve the use of booster rockets.
3. The safety director's decision to revise the safety procedures was based on a recent inspection of the plant.
4. After extensive testing, the physician recommended immediate surgery.
5. The new product, which was developed in two weeks, doubled the company's gross sales.
6. The announcer said, "I'll be back in a minute to tell you how to spend a month in Austria."
7. The director spoke in a harsh voice to the intern. [Or better still: The director spoke harshly to the intern.]

EXERCISE FIVE(B.) Dangling Modifiers - suggested answers

1. After extensive coaching from his campaign manager, the candidate gave a speech that gained him support.
2. Blinded by the approaching car's headlights, John swerved his car off the road into a ditch. [*his car* necessary? Judgment call.]
3. To learn the technique thoroughly, you must [or "one must"] complete the first three exercises.
4. To receive full retirement benefits, employees must participate in the pension plan for 20 years.

5. By reducing each situation to its simplest elements, the analyst discovered the answer.

6. The secretary brought the mail to the director who was sitting at her desk. [No comma would imply that there is more than one director. A comma after the word *director* would imply the one and only director.]

7. By substituting blue for black ink, the printer increased the brochure's visual impact. [Or: "Changing from black to blue ink gave the brochure greater visual impact.]

[Comment by JDB: If this were my sentence, I'd say "Changing the color of ink from black to blue gave the brochure greater visual impact." But I realize I'm probably being overly fussy.]

8. My employment counselor suggested I rewrite my resume after I was rejected by three companies. [Or, perhaps better, "After my rejection by three companies, my employment counselor suggested I rewrite my resume.]

9. My supervisor cancelled the project after I had researched it for five months. [Or: "My supervisor cancelled the project after I had spent five months researching it."]

10. If customers use less water for showers and washing, the water authority will be able to meet the demand for water throughout the summer.

11. While I was waiting for a client to return from lunch, the parking meter expired and a policeman ticketed my car. *[JDB Comment: I can't resist this, because I can picture that meter dying before my very eyes. I'd say, "the time on the parking meter ran out . . ."]*

12. To increase sales, salespersons are using computers to place sixty phone calls an hour, (This sounds a bit ugly because "sales" and "salespersons" repeat their sounds right next to each other. How about trying, instead, "Salespersons, to increase their sales, are using computers to place (or "that can place") 60 phone calls an hour.")

13. After waiting six days for the jury to return a verdict, observers became concerned that the trial might end in a hung jury.

14. While on the floor, the Senator was summoned by a page to meet with a group of constituents.
[For those of you unfamiliar with the workings of government, "on the floor" in this case means being present on the floor of the Senate. This sentence is a good example of the passive voice used correctly; presumably, the Senator and the constituents are more important than the page.]

15. While the writer was mowing the lawn, a new idea popped into her head.

EXERCISE SIX. Unnecessary Shifts — suggested answers

1. In order to follow Sunshine Act procedures, include a statement in the Scheduling block.

2. I certainly appreciated the opportunity to meet with you and to introduce you to our staff during your visit.

3. We have reviewed your draft and submit the following comments.

4. The Town Council increased the water rates and imposed a $3.00 charge for water services.

5. Recent problems with loaning equipment have called for tighter controls.

6. Mr. Cochran criticized the loan department and even asked for a new loan officer.

7. Forest fires destroyed thousands of acres of timber as the flames roared through the valley.

   [Did you put "they" where I've used "the flames"? Fine, except someone is going to say, "*They* refers to thousands of acres, not to forest fires."]

8. The director believes it would be in the manufacturer's interest to report on the initial list as many chemicals as possible.

9. Metro trains were delayed by a malfunctioning signal, causing many commuters to be thirty to forty minutes late for work.

10. Although I was satisfied, I had expected the job to require more imagination. [Or: "Although the job satisfied me, it seemed to require less imagination than I had expected."]

11. [If the instructions are intended for one person] Release the safety catch and then turn the valve. [If the operator is another person:] Release the safety catch; then the operator will turn the valve.

12. A frequent source of complaints was the difficulties encountered in registration. [If this sounds awkward, reverse the order: Difficulties in registration were a frequent source of complaints.]

13. Before starting your own business, you should decide how much money the business requires. [The sentence would be stronger if it were more specific. Does the writer mean the money needed to *open* the business? Or the amount needed not only to open the business but to pay personal expenses until the business makes a profit?]

14. The possibility of additional federal regulation of airline operations causes concern among airline industry officials.

15. The best way to use the note pads is to check off the cards as they become known. [Or: "The best way to use the note pads is to check off the cards as they become known. As an additional aid, as you check

off each card, use the initials of the player showing it."]

EXERCISE SEVEN. The Simple Word—Suggested Answers and Tips

1. Follow the publications division's new rules (being put into effect today) and use simple words. [The phrase shown in parentheses is a "judgment call" here; use it if you think it's needed for precision.]
2. Simple, straightforward writing will help your readers to understand.
3. The price of the ballpoint pen was more than five dollars. [Prefer "more than" to "over" in the sense of being higher. Save "over" and "above" for physical positions. The phrase "more than" emphasizes contrast; "over" and "above" do not.]
4. As the customers waited in line, the clerks gossiped at the register. [Did you catch the SHIFT IN TENSE?]
5. The grass is always greener...[Just checking to see if you're awake.]
7. The accident occurred on the beltway (or circumferential highway). ["Circumvential" exemplifies a frequently encountered mistake. Writers sometimes confuse "soundalike" words and choose the wrong one.]
8. A stitch in time...[Gotcha? We hope not.]
9. The author took his typewriter to the repair shop to be cleaned.
10. The moon cast a golden glow on the clear (surface of the) lake. ["Iridescence" connotes the shimmering qualities of a rainbow; the sun's rays would be a more likely source of an iridescent effect.]

EXERCISE EIGHT(A.) Unnecessary Repetition — suggested answers

1. One of the clerk's responsibilities is the compiling of time and attendance reports. These go to the branch chief, who verifies that the information is accurate and complete.

2. Next year's proposed budget needs to be revised before being released to the public. Otherwise it may draw sharp criticism, because it is not zero-based.

3. Mr. Jensen received the following ratings: Excellent, 21; Good, 5; and Poor, 0.

4. The information obtained from the study should be reported to the

committee by June 23rd. All information should be complete; any that is not should be clearly marked "Incomplete."

5. Although industry officials view the proposed regulations as unnecessary, they are less opposed to them than to the ones proposed last year.

EXERCISE EIGHT(B.) Elegant Variation – suggested answer

Each owner of an automobile is required to register it within 30 days of the time it was purchased. The owner must report the automobile's serial number, engine number, make, and model. The owner must also indicate whether the automobile is used for business purposes. Finally, the owner must indicate whether the automobile was purchased from a recognized dealer. No unlicensed personal automobile will be permitted to operate.

EXERCISE NINE. Parallel Construction – suggested answers

1. Save gasoline by avoiding jack-rabbit starts, maintaining an even speed, and looking ahead to anticipate signal changes.
2. I would like to learn the following from this book:
   1) How to start writing;
   2) How to punctuate;
   3) How to develop style.
3. See immediate returns from the course through greater filing efficiency, quicker insurance claims processing, and improved account collections.
4. Four methods of providing company training are
   - three-day seminars
   - correspondence courses
   - private consultants
   - in-house seminars
5. Please observe the following regulations:
   - Equipment must be reserved two weeks ahead;
   - Equipment may not be removed without being signed out;
   - Equipment must be returned within 48 hours of use.

[Or why not strengthen the whole construction by putting the regulations in the active voice—imperative mood.]

- Reserve equipment two weeks ahead;
- Sign out equipment before removing it from the storage room
- Return equipment within 48 hours.]

6. "I have nothing to offer but blood, toil, tears, and sweat."

7. The manager described the department's problems succinctly, clearly, and candidly.

8. Reviewing the records daily is as important as collecting accurate information.

9. Charles Jarvis is an excellent lecturer, personable conversationalist, and fine writer.

10. "With malice toward none; with charity for all; with firmness in the right, . . . let us strive on to finish the work we are in: to bind up the nation's wounds; to care for him who shall have borne the battle; . . . to do all which may achieve and cherish a just and lasting peace among ourselves, and with all nations." [Sound familiar? it's from Lincoln's Second Inaugural Address. Notice how effectively the parallel structure moves the message along.]

Exercise Ten (A.) Orderly Arrangement - hints and tips

There are probably at least a dozen different ways to rewrite this exercise. Accordingly, we aren't going to give you a "suggested answer" here; instead, we'll give you a few hints and tips that will help you tell whether your own version is a good one, and perhaps enable you to make it even better.

Make use of all the principles you've learned so far. [If you are alert, you may be wondering right now why we didn't simply say "use" instead of "make use." Think about it, please. Our word choice here is deliberate, and we made it because there is a shade of difference we feel it's important to express. Precision!]

Read all the way through before you start to edit or rewrite. Be systematic. Look for passive voice [...has been made...], smothered verbs [...arrived at the determination...], and deadwood [...in accordance with...]. Remedy them if you can; while you're doing that, you'll probably find yourself gaining additional insights on how to improve the arrangement of facts.

Is the information presented in parallel fashion? Is the order logical? [Make sure you don't express copying speed in terms of "number per minute" for one machine and "a copy every X seconds" for another.]

Is exactly the same information presented for each machine? If not, readers may become uncomfortable about the omissions, even if they aren't consciously aware of them.

Is the order logical? That is, have you chosen a scheme of presentation based on, say, alphabetical order? Or price? Or speed of operation?

Would the material be easier to understand if presented in tabular form? Maybe you'd like to try it both ways. [And, since some readers are "word-oriented" and some are "engineering-oriented," you might even consider using both a narrative and an illustrative tabular chart.]

If you still feel the need for more help, we suggest you go back and carefully re-read pages 72 and 73.

Once you've done all this, you're ready for the final test. Put yourself in the reader's shoes. Try to read the rewrite as if you had never seen it before. Does it answer all your questions? Would it make it easy for you to make a decision if you were buying a copying machine? We devoutly hope so.

EXERCISE TEN(B.) Orderly Arrangement — correct order

10, 4, 13, 6, 16, 8, 14, 1, 2, 17, 11, 18, 9, 3, 5, 15, 7, 12

EXERCISE TEN(C.) Writing Instructions — suggested answer

If your answer came out approximately like this, you're on the right track. There may be some minor variations; some of the choices are strictly judgment calls.

Step 1. Write an opening paragraph . . .
Step 2. Divide the process into distinct steps.
Step 3. Present each step in its normal order.
Step 4. Check for and eliminate uncommon words [judgment call]
Step 5. *Show* the reader . . . [judgment call]
Step 6. Check to see that language and nomenclatures . . .
Step 7. If necessary, divide the text . . .
Step 8. Go through all the steps to see . . .
Step 9. Rewrite, rewrite, rewrite . . .

Bibliography

Style Manuals

For private industry, corporate executives, publishers, etc., the most respected style manual is undoubtedly

A Manual of Style (12th Edition, Revised), University of Chicago Press, 1969.

For government employees, your usage "Bible" is

GPO Style Manual, U.S. Government Printing Office, Washington, D. C., 1973.

Writers in the armed services should also be familiar with the GPO Manual. In addition, I would recommend (for all services)

Guide for Air Force Writing (AF Pamphlet 13-2), Department of the Air Force, Headquarters, U.S. Air Force, Washington, D. C., 1 November 1973.

For students, it would be a good idea for you to have a look at all three of the above, plus this very valuable and inexpensive guide:

Turabian, Kate L., *A Manual for Writers of Term Papers, Theses, and Dissertations,* Chicago: University of Chicago Press, 1973.

Now that these basic references are taken care of, the rest of the bibliography is in straight alphabetical order:

Baker, Sheridan, *The Practical Stylist,* New York: Thomas Y. Crowell Company, 1962.
Barzun, Jacques, *Simple and Direct,* New York: Harper & Row, 1975.
Barzun, Jacques, *On Writing, Editing, and Publishing,* Chicago: The University of Chicago Press, 1971.
Bernstein, Theodore M., *The Careful Writer: A Guide to English Usage,* New York: Atheneum, 1967.
Bernstein, Theodore M., *Miss Thistlebottom's Hobgoblins,* New York: Farrar, Straus and Giraux, 1971.
Bernstein, Theodore M., *Reverse Dictionary,* New York: Quadrangle/ The New York Times Book Co., 1975.

Bernstein, Theodore M., *Watch Your Language*, Manhasset, New York: Channel Press, 1968.

Birk, Newman P. and Genevieve B., *Understanding and Using English, (Third Edition with Readings)*, New York: The Odyssey Press, Inc., 1959.

Brusaw, Charles T., Gerald J. Alred and Walter E. Olin, *The Business Writer's Handbook*, New York: St. Martin's Press, 1975.

Burnam, Tom, *The Dictionary of Misinformation*, New York: Ballantine Books, 1975.

Chomsky, Noam, *Reflections on Language*, New York: Pantheon Books, 1975.

Cottam, Keith M. and Robert W. Pelton, *Writer's Research Handbook*, South Brunswick and New York: A.S. Barnes and Company, 1977.

DeBono, Edward, *Wordpower*, New York: Harper Colophon Books, 1977.

Ehrlich, Eugene and Daniel Murphy, *Basic Grammar for Writing*, New York: McGraw Hill Book Company, 1967.

Evans, Bergen and Cornelia, *A Dictionary of Contemporary American Usage*, New York: Random House, 1957.

Evans, Bergen, collected and arranged with comments by, *Dictionary of Quotations*, New York: Delacorte Press, 1968.

Flesch, Rudolph, *Say What You Mean*, New York: Harper and Row Publishers, Inc., 1972.

Flesch, Rudolph, *The Art of Plain Talk*, New York: Collier Books, 1962.

Flesch, Rudolph, *The Art of Readable Writing*, New York: Harper and Row, 1949.

Follett, Wilson, *Modern American Usage*, New York: Hill and Wang, 1966.

Fowler, H. W., *A Dictionary of Modern English Usage*, Kingsport Tenn.: Oxford University Press, 1944.

Fowler, H. W. and F. G., *The King's English (Third Edition)*, London: Oxford University Press, 1931 (issued as paperback, 1973).

Funk, Charles Earle, *Heavens to Betsy!*, New York: Warner Paperback Library, 1972.

Gowers, Sir Ernest, *Plain Words*, New York: Alfred A. Knopf, 1954.

Graves, Robert and Alan Hodge, *The Reader Over Your Shoulder*, New York: The MacMillan Co., 1961.

Gunning, Robert, *The Technique of Clear Writing*, New York: McGraw Hill, 1952.

Guthrie, L. O., *Factual Communication*, New York: The Macmillan Company, 1948.

Hicks, Tyler G., *Writing for Engineering and Science*, New York: McGraw Hill, 1961.

Hodges, John C. and Mary E. Whitten, *Harbrace College Handbook (7th Ed.)*, New York: Harcourt Brace Jovanovich, Inc., 1970.

Irmscher, William F., *The Holt Guide to English*, New York: Holt, Rinehart and Winston, Inc., 1972.

Jones, Virgil Carrington, *Gray Ghosts and Rebel Raiders*, New York: Holt, 1956.

Jones, W. Paul, *Writing Scientific and Technical Reports*, Dubuque, Iowa: Wm. C. Brown Company Publishers, 1971.

Kidner, John, *The Kidner Report (revised edition)*, Washington, D.C.: Acropolis Books Ltd., 1975

Kierzek, John M. and Walter Gibson, *The MacMillan Handbook of English (4th Ed.)*, New York: The MacMillan Company, 1960.

Kredenser, Gail, *Write It Right*, New York: Barnes & Noble Books, Division of Harper & Row, Publishers, 1968.

Lefcowitz, Allan B., *The Writer's Handbook*, Englewood Cliffs, N. J.: Prentice-Hall, Inc., 1976.

Linton, Calvin D., *Effective Revenue Writing 2, Training No. 129 (rev. 7-62)*, Washington, D. C., U.S. Government Printing Office, 1962.

McCarthy, Colman, *Inner Companions*, Washington, D.C.: Acropolis Books, Ltd., 1975.

McCullo, Marion, *Proofreader's Manual*, New York: Richards Rosens Press Inc., 1969.

Martin, Phyllis, *Word Watcher's Handbook*, New York: David McKay Company, Inc., 1977.

Menning, J. H. and C. W. Wilkinson, *Communicating Through Letters and Reports (4th Ed.)*, Homewood, Ill.: Richard D. Irwin, Inc., 1967.

Mitchell, John H., *Writing for Technical and Professional Journals*, New York: John Wiley & Sons, Inc., 1968.

Morris, William and Mary, *Harper Dictionary of Contemporary Usage*, New York: Harper & Row, 1975.

Morsberger, Robert E., *Commonsense Grammar and Style, 2nd Ed.*, New York: Thomas Y. Crowell Company, 1975.

Moore, Robert Hamilton, *Handbook of Effective Writing,* New York: Holt, Rinehart and Winston, 1966.

Mueller, Robert Kirk, *Buzzwords,* New York: Van Nostrand Reinhold Company, 1974.

Newman, Edwin, *A Civil Tongue,* New York: Warner Books, 1977.

Newman, Edwin, *Strictly Speaking,* New York: Warner Books, 1974.

Nicholson, Margaret, *A Dictionary of American English Usage,* based on Fowler's *Modern English Usage,* New York: Signet Books (by arrangement with Oxford University Press, Inc.), 1959.

O'Brien, Robert and Joanne Soderman, *The Basic Guide to Research Sources,* New York: A Mentor Book — New American Library, 1975.

Opdycke, John B., *Harper's English Grammar,* New York: Popular Library (Harper & Row), 1965.

Payton, Geoffrey (compiled by), *The Merriam-Webster Pocket Dictionary of Proper Names,* New York: Pocket Books, 1972.

Perlmutter, Jerome H., *A Practical Guide to Effective Writing,* New York: Delta Books, Dell Publishing Company, 1965.

Pirsig, Robert M., *Zen and the Art of Motorcycle Maintenance,* New York: Bantam Books, 1974.

Pitkin, Walter B., *The Art of Useful Writing,* New York: Whittlesey House, McGraw Hill Book Co., Inc., 1940.

Rivers, William L., *Finding Facts,* Englewood Cliffs, N. J.: Prentice-Hall, 1975.

Rivers, William L., *Writing: Craft and Art,* Englewood Cliffs, N. J.: Prentice-Hall, Inc., 1975.

Roberts, Paul, *English Sentences,* New York: Harcourt, Brace & World, 1962.

Shaw, Harry, *Punctuate It Right!,* New York: Barnes & Noble Books, 1963.

Sheppard, Mona, *Plain Letters,* Washington, D. C.: U.S. Government Printing Office, 1955.

Shostak, Jerome, *Concise Dictionary of Current American Usage,* New York: Washington Square Press, Inc., 1968.

Strunk, William, Jr., and E. B. White, *The Elements of Style,* 2d Ed., New York: MacMillan Publishing Co., Inc., 1972.

Turner, David R., *English Grammar and Usage for Test-Takers,* New York: Arco Publishing Company, 1976.

Willis, Hulon, *Structure, Style, Usage: A Guide to Expository Writing,* New York: Holt, Rinhart and Winston, 1964.

Wincor, Richard, *Contracts in Plain English,* New York: McGraw Hill, Inc., 1976.

Wykoff, George S. and Harry Shaw, *The Harper Handbook, 4th Ed.,* New York: Harper & Row, 1969.

Ziegler, Isabelle, *The Creative Writer's Handbook (2d Ed.).* New York: Barnes & Noble Books, a Division of Harper & Row, Publishers, 1975.

Additional Bibliography For The Third Edition

Brady, John, *The Craft of Interviewing,* Cincinnati: Writer's Digest Books, 1976.

Buzan, Tony, *Use Both Sides of Your Brain,* New York: E.P. Dutton, Inc., 1974 (paperback edition 1976).

Copperud, Roy H., *American Usage and Style: The Consensus,* New York: Van Nostrand, Reinhold Co., 1980.

Cottle, Basil, *The Plight of English,* New Rochelle, N.Y.: Arlington House, 1975.

Crawford, Tad, *The Writer's Legal Guide,* New York: Hawthorn Books, Inc., 1977.

Dean, Leonard F., Walker Gibson, and Kenneth D. Wilson, *The Play of Language,* New York: Oxford University Press, 1971.

Elbow, Peter, *Writing Without Teachers,* London, New York: Oxford University Press, 1973.

Eschholz, Payl A., Alfred F. Rosa, and Virginia P. Park (edited by) *Language Awareness,* New York: St. Martin's Press, 1974.

Fries, Charles Carpenter, *The Structure of English,* New York: Harcourt Brace & Co., 1952.

Hersey, John (edited by), *The Writer's Craft,* New York: Alfred A. Knopf, 1974.

Hogan, Robert, and Herbert Bogart, *The Plain Style,* New York: American Book Co., 1967.

Kenin, Richard, and Justin Wintle, *The Dictionary of Biographical Quotations,* New York: Alfred A. Knopf, 1978.

MacCampbell, Donald, *The Writing Business,* New York: Crown Publishers, Inc. 1978.

Mack, Karin, and Skjei, Eric, *Overcoming Writing Blocks,* Los Angeles: J.P. Tarcher, Inc. (distributed by St. Martin's Press, N.Y.), 1979.

Mitchell, Richard (The Underground Grammarian), *Less Than Words Can Say,* Boston: Little, Brown & Co., 1979.

Munson, Gorham, *The Written Word: How to Write for Readers,* New York: Collier Books, 1949 (1st Collier Book edition, 1976).

Pei, Mario, *Doublespeak in America,* New York: Hawthorn Books, Inc., 1973.

Peter, Dr. Laurence J., *Peter's Quotations: Ideas for Our Time,* New York: Bantam Books, 1979.

Sheehan, Paul D. *Repertorial Writing,* Radnor, Pa.: Chilton Book Co., 1972.

Sisson, A.F., *Sisson's Word and Expression Locater,* West Nyack, N.Y.: Parker Publishing Co., 1956.

Venolia, Jan, *Write Right!* Woodland Hills, Calif: Periwinkle Press, 1979.

Webb, Robert A. (compiled and edited by), *The Washington Post Desk Book on Style,* New York: McGraw-Hill Book Company, 1978.

Wermuth, Paul C., *Modern Essays on Writing and Style,* New York: Holt, Rinehart & Winston, Inc., 1964, 1969.

Zinsser, William, *On Writing Well: An Informal Guide to Writing Nonfiction,* New York: Harper & Row, 1980.

Index

JEFFERSON D. BATES has almost 30 years of experience in writing, editing and all phases of publications management at top levels of government and industry. He was editorial director of the pioneering Air Force "Effective Writing Program" in the fifties. Then for a decade he headed a staff of writers at the National Aeronautics and Space Administration. Bates has ghostwritten speeches and articles for top NASA officials, members of the House and Senate Space Committees, and for every "flight" astronaut from Project Mercury to Skylab. Recently he has been asked to prepare a special program: helping personnel of a federal regulatory agency to apply precise writing techniques in the rule-making process.

Bates is the president of Hampton, Bates & Associates, Inc., consultants in professional communication skills. He has been teaching seminars in Effective Writing since 1968 to a clientele that has included many government agencies, corporations, trade associations, and colleges and universities throughout the country.

He is now at work on several more books, including *ZERC BASE GOBBLE-DYGOOK II, How to Comply with the New PLAIN ENGLISH LAWS.*

 ACROPOLIS BOOKS Ltd.
Washington D.C. 20009